Mt. Juliet
High School Library

HOW THE WAR
IN THE STREETS
IS WON

Books by

GERALD EARLY

Tuxedo Junction: Essays on American Culture   (1989)

"My Soul's High Song": The Collected Works of Countee Cullen, Voice of the Harlem Renaissance   (editor)   (1991)

Speech and Power: The African-American Essay and Its Cultural Content, from Polemics to Pulpit, Vols. 1 and 2   (editor)   (1992-1993)

Lure and Loathing: Essays on Race, Identity, and the Ambivalence of Assimilation   (editor)   (1993)

The Culture of Bruising: Essays on Prizefighting, Literature, and Modern American Culture   (1994)

Daughters: On Family and Fatherhood   (1994)

How the War in the Streets Is Won: Poems on the Quest of Love and Faith   (1995)

HOW THE WAR
IN THE STREETS
IS WON

Poems on the Quest of Love and Faith

by

Gerald Early

TIME BEING BOOKS®
POETRY IN SIGHT AND SOUND

Copyright © 1995 by Gerald Early

All rights reserved under International and Pan-American Copyright Conventions. No part of this book shall be reproduced in any form (except by reviewers for the public press) without written permission from the publisher:

Time Being Books®
10411 Clayton Road
Saint Louis, Missouri 63131

Time Being Books® is an imprint of Time Being Press®
Saint Louis, Missouri

Time Being Press® is a 501(c)(3) not-for-profit corporation.

Time Being Books® volumes are printed on acid-free paper, and binding materials are chosen for strength and durability.

Library of Congress Cataloging-in-Publication Data:

Early, Gerald Lyn.
   How the war in the streets is won : poems on the quest of love and faith / by Gerald Early. — 1st ed.
     p.   cm.
   ISBN 1-56809-003-X (hardcover) — ISBN 1-56809-004-8 (paperback)
   1. Afro-Americans — Poetry. I. Title.
PS3555.A6927H68   1995
811'.54 — dc20
                                                                              95-727
                                                                                 CIP

Cover by Tony Tharenos and Lori Loesche
Book design and typesetting by Lori Loesche
Manufactured in the United States of America

First Edition, first printing (April 1995)

Acknowledgments

The author would like to thank the editors of *Northwest Review, American Poetry Review, Literary Review, River Styx, Black American Literature Forum, Wind, Prairie Schooner, Negative Capability, Obsidian II, Seneca Review, Raccoon,* and the *Chronicle of Higher Education* for featuring various versions of many of these poems in their publications.

"The Green Fields of America," "The Cure," and "With Linnet and Rosalind at the Pacific Ocean" are from *Daughters: On Family and Fatherhood,* © 1994 by Gerald Early. Reprinted by permission of Addison-Wesley Publishing Company, Inc.

One of my dearest literary friendships is with a poet named Ken McClane at Cornell University. If I had not known him and read his poetry over the years, I doubt if this book would have been possible. Ken taught me, through his poetry and his example, how to read poetry and how to go back to it. Shakespeare, Milton, Rilke, Wallace Stevens, Gwendolyn Brooks, Amiri Baraka (as a sixteen-year-old, I read "Black Dada Nihilimus" every day for an entire summer and was struck dumb by it each time), Mark Strand, and newer poets like Dorianne Laux and Carl Phillips, continue to teach me to read. Perhaps this book is a tribute to their teaching me how to read and how to return to what I have read to read anew. I am thankful.

In memory of my grandfather,
Ebeneezer Fernandez,
a strong man and a good Christian

and

In memory of my grandmother,
Melissa Fernandez,
the only politician I ever admired

Every Christian one day reaches the point where he too must be ready to accompany the Master into destruction and oblivion: into that which the world considers folly, that which for his own understanding is incomprehensible, for his own feeling intolerable. Whatever it is to be: suffering, dishonor, the loss of loved ones or the shattering of the work of a lifetime, this is the decisive test of his Christianity. Will he shrink back before the ultimate depths, or will he be able to go all the way and thus win his share of the life of Christ.

— from *The Lord*, Romano Guardini

Contents

Preface

Part One: How the War in the Streets Is Won

How the War in the Streets Is Won   *21*
Below Zero on the Installment Plan   *22*
Cock-fight   *24*
The Quality of Being Poor   *25*
The Kings of Dead Box   *26*
Flamingo, or the Making of Salad   *28*
As Long As You're Living   *30*
Standards Vol. 1   *31*
Lesson on the Clavichord   *32*
Talk Radio, or What the Herd Hears   *33*
Ordering Clothes from a Mail-Order Catalogue   *34*
Voice   *35*
Without Speech   *36*
Halloween   *37*
Amphibian   *38*
In the Living Room   *39*
The Green Fields of America (Paths of Our Republic)   *41*

Part Two: Prizefighting and the Modern World

Prizefighting and the Modern World   *45*
Piccolo, or the Culture of Bruising   *46*
The Autobiographies of Ex-Colored Men, Part I   *47*
The Autobiographies of Ex-Colored Men, Part II   *48*
The Autobiographies of Ex-Colored Men, Part III   *50*
Satyagraha   *51*
Soon, One Morning: The Last Stand of Andy Bowen   *53*

Part Three: The Art of the Chest

Tribute to the Art of the Chest   *57*
Old Dirt Road   *58*
Ulysses As the King of Spades   *59*
Chief Crazy Horse Meets Caliban   *60*
Bobby Timmons' Live Soulful Jazz   *62*
The Fire-Eater, or the Engaged Artist As Miracle Monger   *63*
Amagideon, or When Lee Andrews and the Hearts Sang
   Only for Me   *64*

Stairway to the Stars   *67*
Innocency, or Not Song X   *68*
D.W. Griffith's Picture in the Papers, or Room for Romance   *70*
Specific Jazz, or How Birdland Got Its Name   *71*
Lawrence Talbot: King of the B-Movies   *73*
The Dreadful Bop of Flyers   *74*
Country or Western Music   *78*
The Lonesome Death of Sam Cooke   *80*
A Ghost Writer's Song in Remembrance of Romance   *81*
The Staff Writer's Quest for an Historical Yardbird   *85*
Four Songs at the End of Winter   *86*
Swing to the Many   *89*
Diet of Worms   *90*
James Baldwin at the Apollo Theater, 1968   *91*

Part Four: Consensus Vessels

Consensus Vessels   *95*
The Art of Chess   *97*
Grooveyard   *98*
Occasional Rain   *100*
Why Isn't Marseille Said the Way It Looks?   *101*
Pragmatism, or Jehovah's Witnessing   *102*
The Cure   *104*
Thurifer   *106*
Some Memories of an American Girlhood   *107*
Dumbo's Ears, or How We Begin   *108*
Listening to Frank Sinatra   *109*
Destry Rides Again   *111*
Five Études and a Jeremiad   *112*
With Ida at the Pacific Ocean   *114*
With Linnet and Rosalind at the Pacific Ocean   *115*
Teaching Contemporary African-American Literature   *116*
Lear and His Daughter   *117*
With Linnet and Rosalind at the Mouth of the Mississippi   *119*
Lighter Than Air   *120*
Sussex Carol   *121*

Preface

I am known largely, perhaps almost exclusively, as an essayist and a cultural critic — in short, as a writer of prose. Some may be startled, then, to see a book of my poetry, but I have written poetry far longer than I have prose. Indeed, when I was younger, during my undergraduate days, I thought I would be first a poet, then a novelist. I even won several of the English Department awards for undergraduate poetry while a student at the University of Pennsylvania, although I hardly consider them marks of distinction, grateful as I am to have received them. Poetry came to take more and more of a back seat in my writing career, especially when I was working toward my Ph.D., as I studiously and self-consciously began to develop my style as an essayist.

Nonetheless, I continued writing poetry regularly during my early years as an assistant professor as a kind of shorthand for my essays. That is to say, I was getting more ideas for essays than I could actually write, so I would write a poem on the subject as a marker to come back to it later to make an essay of it. Few of the poems ever became essays except some of the early pieces I wrote about my children, which eventually were, in some measure, reworked as the book called *Daughters*. When I began to get some of these poems published, I was momentarily amused then disconcerted. I had a reputation to protect at this point, and it became obsessively important that my poetry could not be seen in the literary public's eye as being in any way "less" than my prose. This made poetry writing more stressful, more arduous, more neurotically driven, as I felt I was taking more risks with it, could afford fewer mistakes. I decided to avoid, in all manner, any of the networking and politicking in literary circles to build a public reputation as a poet, so that the poetry had the appearance of being a "casual" product. This was a cause of some considerable mental relief. But there was, buried in this "casual" attitude, a sense of great daring, a far greater demand of discipline and harsh testing than the essays have ever been. I remember that Charles Mingus, the great jazz bassist, made a solo-piano album (back during the days when such albums were relatively rare even for professional jazz pianists). It was, this cocky effort, a strenuous challenge, not of jazz pianists exactly (although Mingus saw it that way) but of Mingus himself, of what sort of psychic blood and treasure he was willing to expend to make himself a better musician. This book might be seen in something like that light: an attempt to pay the price to be a better writer.

I have continued to write poetry over the years. In fact, I have worked, in some sense, even harder at developing a self-conscious style and range of subject matter for my poems than for my prose. Unlike my essays, the poems here try to do a great deal in harnessing a kind of expressive, compact power within the frame of an especially circumscribed set of images, figures, and symbols. When I write an essay, I am trying very hard to expand, to break boundaries, to defy, at times, continuity. With poetry, I work very hard with the idea of constriction, of working within a very tight space. In this sense, the poems are connected, and each speaks to the other. My essays do this as well but in a less obvious and necessary way.

In part, my need to work harder as a poet is because of the pressure of being a "black" poet, that is, a racially self-conscious artist, or, more precisely, my need to exert an equal pressure against being constricted or told to conform.

I am not sure what being a black poet is supposed to mean, and on one level it is scarcely possible and surely not desirable for me to be anything else. On the other hand, I do not write explicitly "racial" poetry or explicitly "political" poetry either, although I suppose, in its way, the poetry is "racial" enough and "political" enough, as I think all good art or all art aspiring to be good should speak about the artist and his or her vision of the world, and part of myself and part of my vision of the world is surely racial — alas, an acknowledgment that is made less as an assertion of self-determination than a nod to sheer helplessness. In that sense, I am a black poet in much the same way that someone is a Jewish poet or a woman poet or an American Indian poet.

While I imagine that many of the poems in this book could not have been written by a white poet, they also could not have been written by any other black poet either. Like Countee Cullen, the great Harlem Renaissance poet, who was black, I would like to be thought of as a poet, period, and it gives little comfort to me to be slotted, so to speak, as a black poet by either whites or blacks. The poems here will not be augmented or given any deeper merit by calling me a black poet. Being black certainly does not explain why these poems came into being or why they are what they are, although I will be the first to claim, eagerly so, that these poems arise, in part, from a black literary tradition, a black tradition in the symbolic reading of the world. But that is far from being the only tradition that informs them or the only tradition with which they seek association. The poems are likely to be diminished by viewing them racially, reducing both the author and the reader in one fell swoop, each trapped in a labyrinth of expectations and evasions that corrupts and imprisons while, hideously, granting the illusion of liberation and judgment and will. To my black readers, I say simply that this is not a question of racial pride or racial loyalty, and I no more want to be known as a black poet than the late Ralph Ellison would wish to be known as a "black" National Book Award winner or Randall Cunningham as a "black" quarterback or the late Miles Davis as a "black" trumpeter. To be black, a categorization of infinite mirth, finite merit, and absurd inconvenience, is not an aspiration or a state of being. It is not what I am or hope to be. It is, in its complexity, a set of propositions, limitations, and denials that I must master. To my white readers, I say simply that I will gladly take the title of "black" poet when Euro-American poets are pleased and find it necessary to call themselves "white" poets and their work "white" poetry. I am under no illusions about a "color-blind" world that certainly does not now exist. I desire no hiding place from being black and could not have one even if I did. But I wish, not unreasonably, in the matter of being read, to be no more burdened by race than any white writer is. This is not special pleading but simply a call for common respect.

Gerald Early
November 6, 1994
St. Louis, Missouri

HOW THE WAR
IN THE STREETS
IS WON

I want to be an honest man and a good writer.
— from *Notes of a Native Son*, James Baldwin

Part One

How the War in the Streets Is Won

* This symbol is used to indicate that a stanza has been divided because of pagination.

How the War in the Streets Is Won

(for my cousin, murdered on the streets of Philadelphia by his brothers)

> *In the end, I was love.*
> — Gene McDaniel's and Bobby Hutcherson's "Now"

Casting his head down he saw, in the empty closet,
Tossed in a corner, forgotten, hidden from the light,
Almost like uprooted things, two shoes, black and silver, shiny,
Polished, leathered and lean, sharp and cheap: a cornerboy's shoes.
He gently removed the shoes, nearly new, from the darkness of the
    closet
To the light of the room outside, felt the greasy gleam
And thought to himself: These were hardly worn, hardly broken in.
Inside the shoe he felt a certain stiffness, a narrow, thin
Resistance to the feet that seemed to grow as wide as an ox's back.
Who could wear such preposterous shoes, such pathetic eloquence
That swells so deep as seems to say that the world which will not
    hear,
That such a world is best left to the devices of its silence?
He thought instantly about the boy running down the street,
Who, as soon as the bullet hit his brain, narrowing his eyes,
Rushing rapidly to the ground, thought quickly, I'm dead. How so?
O such a silly boy, he remembered, dropping the shoes in the empty
    closet,
Hearing the resounding echo there as if it were coming from Penuel;
The boy he walked arm in arm with, together imagining
The moves they could make in the street *diddly, diddly, sh'bop,*
As cool as anything alive, when they would finally be old enough
To buy and stroll in a pair of movables such as those wonders in the
    closet.

Below Zero on the Installment Plan

Slouching pantaloons and eyes, and sagging coat
And eyes, and burnt-out days and burnt-out eyes,
And flying loons and eyes, and eyes as if popped
Eyes were not eyes at all but were the accompaniment

Of clothes, of disarray on the arms, specks and pits,
So exquisite that it resembles nothing so much as
A bad heart, a heart gone uniquely wrong, a common ill,
A heart so broken that it scarcely knows what broken is.

She thinks that today someone will come to take her TV,
The one laser of light, marvel of science, that tells her
It's today she lives in and not the misery of any time on record;
And that someone will take her children, one by one,

To live with someone else who pays bills on time,
Who does not wait in line for money orders, who does
Not stand in the middle of the marketplace turning in circles.
So she peers over the railing, down the maze of stairs,

Twisting down like a coiling dizziness, a coiling darkness,
And while looking down tries not to remember a dry, slow
Wind that swept the bed, her breasts, thinking the while,
"Has he come yet? Must there be more than this?" turning her head

As she tries not to remember hearing a baby scream and scream
And tries not to see, in one's cracked-up dream of white
Water and roses, its scarlet skin bubble like peeling paint
In boiling water as she tried to move to stop it, to take

The baby away but felt her bones ache and wither, her eyes turn
   down.
So she sits herself there on the landing holding a broken lipstick,
Two other children beyond the open doorway watching TV as
You watch two men climb up, dressed to kill, walking casually

As if walking to a café in Paris on a warm, golden evening;
They wear sunglasses. Ah, the sweet array of the finely clothed!
Their extraordinary rose-colored shoes rich like wine in a glass,
Glowing in the darkness like something other than roses, other than
   shoes.

The dry, slow wind blows down the hall across her fingers and face;
A boy walks by, staring in her face, her dark, popped eyes, jumping
As she awaits that tantalizing white scent of white water the men
   wear,
So much like the pretty rush and wave you hear and feel before you
   drown.

Cock-fight

(a Filipino in California during the Great Depression)

One afternoon, like a kind of gesture that
Comes about when there is nothing better
To do, he placed his very dark brown arm
Quite, quite next to her very white one, and
Thought this, naturally, a very laughable comparison.
Because, he noticed, his hands, despite his work,
Seemed almost pretty and softer than hers, which
Were so very, very white and should have been soft.
He thought of this every night with her white arms
Encircling his quite, quite brown back, her big blond face —
Not a sweet face, as it were, but so very, very blond
That if blondness were a virtue, it would have been sweetness.
He thought of this on this very night with his prizefighting
Red and white cock, his extravagant animal, under his arm,
As he lifted her suitcase from the porch and turned to see
Her father, grim and darkly, standing there, so poised behind
His blue-cold rifle as to seem a statue standing there waiting for
Some other gesture to signify that standing there was some kind
Of grand and grim work of art; so like something carved he was.
A darting, licking tongue of red flashed out, and, as it did so,
Her very white arm and his quite brown arm came up,
Each to shield the other as if from a tremendous blow. Up
The arms came as he grunted, and she yelled out, and he
Fell backward, and up from his other arm flew the stricken
Cock and down the porch steps fell the suitcase as he and she
Watched the flailing cock, wounded and dying, and the blizzard
Of white feathers as if neither had, in their entire lives, seen snow
   before.

The Quality of Being Poor

(to the boys of my past who have died from drug addiction and street-gang wars and to those who have gone to prison)

How nice to wear the heavy and full coat
when the ground is very hard and cold,
the bars cold, the air buzzing with
an echo of birds that sound spooky
there like gulls over a dark cemetery.
No one was there anymore and nothing,
not even a torn swing, a rusted slide,
nor a boy there throwing a ball up and down;
when once, looking through the bars, there
where so many boys, enough to fill a world
up to the brim with mischief and mutterings
of mischief as to keep a heart and soul warm
as wearing a full and heavy coat with such
warmth as makes one shudder of how cold
it used to be there in the playground with
such thin, cheap clothes, such papery coats.
One presses, with a full coat, against the bars
to see such a wonder gone to waste and to wonder
if the world makes boys only to make wretches
in the end; such lushly wrought misery, like
a chirping on the wire that reminds one of
all these absences so that one does not think
of the cold anymore or how cold one used to be
but of how nice it is to wear the heavy coat
and of the golden gulches stretching out across the land.

The Kings of Dead Box

(for Kenny, who died too young, and his brothers, all champions of Dead Box, who, together, made up the divinity of the street corner)

As a boy I thought,
I honestly thought,
I really thought I could walk with a limp to Jerusalem,
That I could walk there
And it would be like walking from some far place,
From some here to some there,
And it would be fun, a boyish kind of fun,
To walk from here to there;
Like walking across the schoolyard
Which was, I thought as a boy, the largest,
The absolute largest space I knew;
And I would walk from east to west
In the schoolyard, from eastgate to westgate,
And that was, would be to my little boy's mind,
Just like, exactly like, walking with a limp to Jerusalem
Because the other gate was Jerusalem and
While walking through the schoolyard
On my way to Jerusalem I would stop for ten minutes
Or so (or something like that) and play Dead Box
With my friends because they were, would not be coming.
They were not going to Jerusalem,
Not walking with a limp, not running,
Just all hunkered down with their clay-filled bottle tops,
Playing Dead Box, going from number to number
Until one could land on the skull and crossbones
And become a killer and kill everyone else's top.
And I thought I could stop for ten minutes
To play Dead Box with my friends and then
Just get up and walk with a limp
The rest of the way to Jerusalem
In my sneakers that were sometimes black, sometimes white.
But I could not walk the distance as a boy,
Not from eastgate to westgate, not so far as that,
Because I could not walk beyond the Dead Box game
And the four or so black boys who were my friends,
Who were my friends and who were playing there.
But I'd like to think as a man
That I could walk that space simple as pie;

Not to Jerusalem, which is too far now to go with a limp,
But the space across the schoolyard,
From eastgate to westgate, and not stop at all now
And still pretend that it is like walking with a limp to Jerusalem.
But halfway there I still see four or so black boys
Playing Dead Box, and I stop and wait to hear them call me.
But they do not call me; yet I want them to call
So I can play Dead Box with them because it
Is really too far to walk from eastgate to westgate
And who wants to walk there really anyway
When one can scuttle across the ground making numbers
And killing tops and pass the time playing Dead Box,
Pass the time playing Dead Box with friends?
But they do not call me at all except, while
I am standing there, one clay-filled top leaves
The square and hits the heel of my brown wingtip shoe.
The top leaves "the mystic square of death," as we once called it,
And hits my wingtip shoe heel and glances off a bit just so.
And then one black boy asks for his top back just so
Because I picked it up, thought it felt a good shooter.
They do not call or notice me again, not even once
After he gets the top back, not even once.
And so I walk back to eastgate because who
Wants to pretend to walk with a limp to Jerusalem anyway?
Who wants to go to Jerusalem alone when one can
With relish play a deadly game with friends?
But, not being royalty anymore, I know that Dead Box is
Really the last blood sport, not of boys, but of kings.

Flamingo, or the Making of Salad

(a poem for parents who have lost young children)

Manna.
She, looking through the window and thinking,
Or seeming to be looking and thinking,
Sees manna fall in the yard.

She remembered the declension of 25
Golden-black orioles, who covered the yard with shit.

(No, he thought, in his room. Try again to get the memory right.)

In remembering the descent of 25
Golden-black orioles, who with shit covered the yard,
Or the descent of 25 or so defecating birds
Named after a baseball team in a town made famous
By some black slave who escaped his bondage.

(I don't think that's right, he convinced himself. The team.
The team is named after the birds. ~~Not.~~ It is
Something like living life to tell about
Some life in some poem such as this. No. It is something else.)

In remembering the descent of 25
Golden-black orioles, who the yard with shit covered,
She realized the doing nothing of her hands
~~And the doing something of the birds; the reaching~~

No, the doing something of the orioles,
Golden-black like the nigger slave and the shitting manna.

And first she turned on the radio to something
Like someone or someones singing what we know,
What we know is something like life:

The movie wasn't so hot.
It didn't have much of a plot.

And then she began the doing something more with
The doing nothing hands by making salad
To put in as the ~~birds were putting out~~

(Ooops, he turned in his chair. Not right. This way:
To put in as the gold-black orioles
Were putting out outside.)

First, break the lettuce to make a bed on the plate.
Then, slice the red onion with a sharp blade slipping.
Then, cucumber, green pepper, celery, carrots, radishes,
Mushrooms, one by one, cut, diced, sliced and scattered
Like like like like . . . well, wait a minute.
(I know! he banged his fist, like lives tossed upon
The ground in an airplane crash.
(I'm sorry. I did not mean that. I wanted only to be funny.
I meant like the pieces of a game tossed by a child . . .
That's worse and not even funny at all. He lights a cigarette.)

The radio plays some song like this:
I know I'm going to love you.
Nothing can stop me, cause I'm the Duke of Earl.
The kind of song she heard as a girl
On a transistor radio, badly out of tune, squawking,
While eating Lay's potato chips by a window.

She cuts tomato, a bit of cheese, adds dressing.

(And then, he remembers something, something he said to her:
"You can't name a child Flamingo; what kind of name is that?"
And she just ate potato chips and sat on the bed and said:
"I'll name this child whatever I want, whatever I feel like.")

And she does ~~a funny thing.~~ an odd thing.

("Oh!" he remembers saying, just "Oh!" like someone clearing his
throat, ~~of someone just~~ . . .)

And she spins, startled when all she heard said was "Oh!"
And with the knife, she slices her hand from end to end,
As pretty as you please and calmly watches the
Mad, mad blood gush everywhere: cutting board, sink, and salad.

("Oh!" he says again, "Oh, dear!" ~~but not the same oh~~)

Such blood as you have never seen from such a simple cut.
It was, you might figure, blood for the little ghost who,
Once unghosted, like a flamingo, used to chase the golden-black
Orioles, shitting, from the tree of mana
While Garnett Mims and the Enchanters sang on the radio.

As Long As You're Living

He closed the book and, as he did so,
He rose, and so the book fell softly
To the ground, fanning open in a
Shower of pages that whitely settled
On some black print which had told him,
While he was reading, the story of a
Woman that made him think of his mother,
Although the woman was not his mother
And she lived long ago and in some other
Place, which he had always wanted to see.
It was the blackness of her skin described
That struck: "Like a plum so full as seemed breaking."
It was his mother's skin, he thought, as rich as that, so
That he wished to escape by letting the book rest where it fell.

Standards Vol. 1

*(for the workers murdered in the National
Super Market in black St. Louis)*

As the detective pushed through the doors,
The opening chords of "Stardust" came to him.
As he walked around the blown blood and bits, looked
At each body lying near the counter where, often,
Welfare checks were cashed and women grunted like swine,
He felt something shudder in his back, saying, *Now you know.*

The song, "Stardust," began to grow in him, strain by
Strain, old Hoagy's tune, as he kneeled among the bodies,
Not even thinking of the strange holocaust here, when
Someone from the neighborhood tapped his shoulder:
"Will they close the store? I can't go no other place."
He could faintly hear a baby's cry, barking, feel the faint half-moon.
"A strange tune," another one spoke up, "to be whistling for the
 dead?"
Startled, he turned, shrugging, "Standards go with anything," he
 said.

Lesson on the Clavichord

(for the Haitian refugees)

Something this student feels about the
Border of a sound that is much like
The border of a country: a silken set
Of cords, a resonance that guards the room,
A kind of sentry that orders the sound
Of suffering, which, on such a soft-sounding
Instrument, can be much like the chords
Of the sound of something other than suffering;
Not even an echo of that but something
Silken like a sonata on an afternoon that
This student is trying to learn to play
With one bandaged finger tapping the keys
With the flat resonance of banging in annoyance
At the bloody finger and the sharp, clumsy pain.

Talk Radio, or What the Herd Hears

What is it, as is said, that one wishes to hear
Come across the wires, come into the room,
Come bidden in the car, a sound to which we lend
A bent ear, curved by that sound, inclined by gossip, of
What is heard there: not hearts singing but simple talk,
A relishing of the common yak and patter,
A dizzying litany of complaints and opinions
That is, like a kind of wealth, the meaning of our time
As we sit bloody cheek by jowl, tongues poised at our noses?
The dial buzzes and squawks, as we do, sputtering,
As we learn that if hearts cannot sing, they,
There, coming across the wires, can certainly talk
Incessantly into the curved ear, and what is heard
Incessantly is (or in) ourselves, bewildered and beleaguered
By the all and everything that seems so much more
Or less than what our words can ever unceasingly say.

Ordering Clothes from a Mail-Order Catalogue

> *"We're looking for zootsuits to burn."*
> — white rioter in Los Angeles, March 1943

It is the world we crave, or think
We crave, for we want less than that,
Less than the miseries or the very heart;
Not the world we want but its luxuries,
An opulent bauble ringing in the ears,
The luxury of the world's unsmudged dreams, the colors:
To be a catcher in a baseball game
Your team wins one to nothing, and
Your pitcher throws a perfect game,
And you are *seen* throwing him high in the air.
It is finally *that* world we want,
A world captured in pictures, in poses,
In postures where everybody seems to move
But no one does, a dance without a false step,
Without a fool who wears the zootsuit in another picture,
Who lies, like those others, in a pool of his own blood
Framed in the fashion of an evening in Los Angeles.
My, what we won't do in the name of fashion!
But there is that other world full of pretty pictures,
Dimly divine daguerreotypes of the sums of souls,
Where a purchase signifies an entrance
To the Meccaland of crisp autumn apples
Being eaten by a cozy fire with a well-dressed, slim, white mate.
What a sort of cooing counsel of well-being it is
To open our book of pictures to the right places
When we untie the bundles and parcels that contain
The fictive merchandise of our fashionable rage.

Voice

(in memory of Raymond Griffin II, five years old, who died of alcohol poisoning)

It is time to return to a sound —
Not a place or time or a desire within
That smolders without a voice — a sound we
Need without place, future or past, a blank art.

(It was, let us say, a warm night, nothing, as it were,
But darkness and a screaming, drunken, dark child
Ripping the wallpaper in terror of the terrors
That, I think, sir, can only be approximated by imagining
Forever going under a forever creeping, deepening sea
Where, waiting at the end, is more darkness and screaming,
Drunken, dark angels, who look for all the world like children,
Who tear their hair, have no voice, are lost, lost, lost,
For the lostness of what hath been done unto them, sir.)

Endlessly, we stand outside to build a drum —
To reach that fullness of something eternally
Human snatched from something eternally inhuman.
Carved wood, a stretched skin, a burning fire, a garbled
Sound we know within that burns like a voice, our voice;
A sound that endlessly announces the darkness, drenching
The voice of that darkness, the voice of the void that,
Upon our senses, o dear darkness, seems such a fire; a
Sound that rises like the morning of an execution, a rising
Bloody tide, like God's speech or the devil's, dinning in our ears.

Without Speech

(for Eugene B., a childhood friend, who was killed in an automobile accident on the Walt Whitman Bridge, which connects Philadelphia to Camden, New Jersey)

It is the one window on the block you notice;
A big bay window that fronts a room of cheap
Furniture, that frames dingy drapes, a
Television that is always on, and one can
Hear, beyond the glass, a melodrama, a comedy.

In the big bay window is a cracking picture,
Cracking from the sunlight, faded to white,
A picture from a photographer's studio, you know,
A study of a young man's face at graduation or
The night of the prom, a face framed by stiff,

Conked hair and wearing a look that you know he
Could not have possessed when, an instant before
The smash, a moment when the utter magic of freak
Occurrence and the blood of pathos stuffs the mouth,
He realized, in that instance of belonging, what, in the picture,

He seemed, in its whiteness, only to be dumbly guessing at.

Halloween

I had forgotten that it was Halloween
And wondered how I could forget what,
As a child, was so thoroughly unforgettable

That I thought of it in March and June
And on my birthday and on Thanksgiving,
When I was wishing it was Halloween

Once more and not some day for dull dinner
And dull talk by dull adults I had not seen
Before and would not, for the life of me,

See again before the next Thanksgiving, when,
Of course, I would be wishing that it was not
Unless it was Christmas, which was worse

For the resurrection of dead relatives and manners
At long dinner tables, and gifts you didn't want
Because they were never as pretty as the picture —

O Christmas, such a Platonist curse, how it hurt
Me so that on Christmas night, in bed, all I could
Do was cry and not think about the next one that was sure

To come quickly; so, I thought of Halloween, when
I was all dressed up as something else, finally
And terribly so much myself that I could, yes,

I could terrorize people into giving me the
Very things I wanted them to give me. I was
Not a child anymore for that one night but something

That only a child could be: a make-believe of my
Own heart. And in that awful adult world, so full
Of awfulness and adults, it was so nice for that

One night not to be a child yet only what a child
Had a right and business being at all: what it would.
But how could I forget so much of that that I,

On the night of nights, must walk to the store to
Get the children treats and be surprised by
Some shapes behind me, dark witches and fair princes,

Ghosts and hosts of monsters, so full of the vanity
Of the dance that only children make and to hear one masked
Voice so oddly say, "Albion," to me, or "Orion," and then all

Skedaddle off and to stand so puzzled, as if it were an Ice
Age of an answer I was waiting for, instead of thinking of
How wonderful it used to feel, disguised to the nines,
To know the secret nonsense of a world that could once afford it.

Amphibian

(for the murdered schoolchildren of Stockton, California)

There is nothing to do but fall on your knees
Because nothing, not any single bone within,
Can keep you standing. Nothing is solid, and
All is air, so to fall on one's knees is only to

Be expected, bowing to the sheer spray of carnage
In a sheer relief that this was, in the end, only
What carnage can be if it is decided that such
Acts will not grow on trees: the screech of our

Dislocation as whitely witnessed as a snowfall.
And everyone thinks, seeing you on your knees, that
You are praying which is, you know, the farthest
Thing from your mind, although everyone likes a good

Prayer after carnage. But a moment comes clearly
Before you when, before this day, comes another day:
A boy tells you (a very little boy) that he wishes
With everything in him that the landscape was full of toads.

Yes, everybody knows about little boys and toads, little
Boys and their love of horrid creatures and hideous mischief.
"But they are so ugly," you say. "But they grow again new,"
He says, something about regeneration, not a word he should know,

As if it were the most self-evident thing that every
Grotesque thing grows itself new so as to give us
So many opportunities to learn that the beauty of
The thing is that the scourge of it is repeated forever

In our ever, everlasting appeal to forgive the scourge
That is so ever, everlastingly in us, the scourge that is us.
So on your knees, all you can think of is the positively
Comfortable, homey feeling of seeing a nuisance boy orchestrating
Endless rows of toads, bumpy and gleaming, as far as the eye can see.

In the Living Room

(for the occasion of left-handed pitcher Herb Score's fall from grace)

Then shall they begin to say to the mountains, Fall on us; and to the hills, Cover us.
— Luke 23:30

When we are watching on the edge
Of our seats with children, waiting,
We know there is a moment that comes
Before *the* moment which we have been promised.

There is a moment that comes, blistering,
Like the most splendid silver,
When we know that some grand act has ended
Or was not really ever acted, like a promise.

But the *other* moment before is when,
Looking at the sky for light, quiet light,
When looking at the sky for the sign of silver,
Someone, some child, asks "What?" again "What?"

"What really is the source of light?"
And as we are edging to the end, the edge,
We do not think at all it is a hard thing
To choose between the silver of the sun or the stars.

And so the child asks again
While we are edging forward for *the* moment,
"What is the source of light here? What is silver?"
And we must say either sun or stars, glory or fractured eternity.

But before we can answer comes *the* moment,
And we have reached the edge of the seat,
And the what we have been awaiting so long arrives.
And we do not think of choices of light anymore.

The moment comes and is gone quickly, splintering dazzle:
A man hits a ball that hits a pitcher in the eye.
The pitcher falls down, falls down the hill;
Almost funny, as if to say in this moment, "Eureka!"

This is how things end. The hills do not fall *on* us;
But we, stumbling, half-blind by the silver promised so hot,
  streaked,
Fall and roll and tumble from them, from the hills, down.
And so it is over like everything else is over:

Just another stricken someone cast down by the light,
Groveling in the dirt, gasping and grasping up.
And it is not the silver of the sun or the stars we think of
But of the god of promises who, without mercy, puts our small light
   out.

It always ends like that, every moment, falling like that,
While we are waiting at the edge of our seats;
So, unexcited, we can answer the child only this when asked
About light and the *other* moment: "Epigone, false Brahma, moon."

The Green Fields of America
(Paths of Our Republic)

> *For everything that lives is holy, life delights in life*
> — William Blake, "America, a Prophecy" (1793)

> *The paths of their way are turned aside.*
> — Job 6:18

Stretched out against a blue, hard, benignly remote sky,
Taut and poised as a dancer's muscled stillness,
As a mouse upon a cat's bare, bloody throat,
As the bloody lines of empire dimly netting the throes,
As the distant church-spire pressed tight against the wire,
Is the season of our joy and pain flung in its dimensions
Of balls and strikes and fouls and errors and outs and pauses,
Boredom and spit, a soft, soft waster of time, the irrelevant
Gallantry of outfielders outstretched for catches: The Game.
And this we watch — o splendid errand — against the blue, hard
    sky,
The men below in a child's game that only, then,
Those men, magically, can play to provide, in grace,
For us, the throng, at last, the will to outlast that sorrow
Against which this dubious contentment is our only flight
To a tremulous childhood of tumultuous peace, that, spoken in the
Tragic speech of prayer, alas, can bring us, rejoicing in that
Regeneration abounding (This, then, the only love that's left
In that stolen expanse of our glory!), fairly struck in the sunlit
Reaches of our grievance and our divine repair.

Part Two

Prizefighting and the Modern World

*Black Boy, O Black Boy,
is the port worth the cruise?*
— from *Harlem Gallery*, Melvin B. Tolson

Prizefighting and the Modern World

Angelically turning his head,
He saw a girl's very indifferent eyes,
Heard the thin cry for his blood upon the floor,
From high and away, his blood on the killing floor;
And he turned his head another way and waited.
Falling down, alas, was the hardest of the two
And not getting up, which, telling himself,
He did so quickly that he could not recall why he fell.
Get up, he told himself, and up he was, like that,
Losing again, staggering again, and waiting for the end
With the heroic benignity of a child watching the moon.
Easy like that it was to get up to get beat up again.
But the falling down was hard, a floppy descent from
Not grace and all that but maintaining, hanging on.
So long to go down and so sweet and peaceful.
He found it hard to believe that the rage that caused
His downfall could make him almost happy, succumbing
To a sleep that passes all understanding.
But he was up again like that, just like that,
Waiting, his face a battered thing, a mask like
The finest sort of perishing, waiting for the end.
No, not this ending: The fights come and go, and go again.
But that ending, some other ending where he could
Imagine Tom Molineaux, weak, spitting blood,
Dying in a dirty bed of filthy linen; other
Negroes in the filthy room come and go, muttering
About the foul end of the foul slave who could not beat Cribb.
And Molineaux angelically turns his head, absolutely
Not sorry to be a wretch, stinking, in the end,
Not praying to some dumb Damballah, not aflame with gnostic
    glory,
But turns his head to his window, the only window there,
And his indifferent eyes stare indifferently on the modern world.
It was, of course, the ending he always imagined
While gasping for air in appeal,
Benighted by shrouds of his own sweat, bored
And enfeebled by his shallow gallantry,
This one moment when the absolute showering
Opulence of certain, positive thinking
Would anoint him with the assurance that,
In the modern world, everything counts but nothing matters.

Piccolo, or the Culture of Bruising

(on seeing a young Roberto Duran train for a prizefight in 1976)

He was, sitting there, his head against the rough rope,
So small and brown that he seemed a boy; no, even more
Than that, he seemed a boy and a girl, a youth without
One strand or strain of sin or darkness in him, a plumed wonder,
Sitting there, on a leaning stool, with bandaged hands, in a gym
Of incensed stench, sweating, eating an ice cream, his head
Tilted slightly sideways and back, so it seemed against the rough
 ring rope.
He looked so much like a youth one might find walking
Upon a beach on a hot day, the sunlight a holy glory gilded
Upon his shoulders; his brown eyes blazed with the dumb
 consciousness
Of dumb youth, silly, playful, the voluptuousness of chastity
 extravagantly etched.
What pain it is to love so much the beauty in this boxer that is not
 there
Because one loves so much and hopes for the beauty that is.
What ordeal to think this vacant angel fulfills our worship,
Answers our prayers for light, is our feeble rescue from our own
 desolation.
He finishes his ice cream, flips the stick away in the air,
And turns to leave the gym, when quickly, cattish tense, he turns
And sends a shower of sizzling spit, which lands like a jet
Upon the shoe of some man who simply looks and glares
And knows, unlike the rest of us, why the spit is there,
Why it edges on the corners on his white leather shoes, bubbly and
 hot.
And the boxer looks as well, his arms poised like some dancer of
Exquisite darkness about to cloak the world in a furious denial of
 light.
The man with the soiled shoes simply looks and then turns away.
The boxer grunts, grabs his penis in disdain, laughs wildly,
And looking so much like some ancient idol of Byzantium, golden
 and hard,
Acknowledges the victory so richly earned and deserved by
He who is so often called, by bodies and souls, our lord of the
 flowers.

The Autobiographies of Ex-Colored Men, Part I

(for boxers Jack Johnson and Joe Louis)

*Take this hammer and carry it to my captain,
And tell him that I'm gone.*
— Mississippi John Hurt

At a white-covered breakfast table
Near a stone-white beach,
Beneath a glowing hot sun, a holiday sun,
Shielded by a huge umbrella
Frayed with gold tassels like epaulets,
Shadow-drenched in white, sits the demigod of the duskies:
Jack Johnson peels tangerines, sips a drink from a white, thin cup,
Waiting, wearing a starched white shirt, stiff
In the breeze like a canvas of pure white darkened by shade.
His Malacca cane slanted on the opposite chair,
A pure Persian cat upon his lap, surveying with her master
The passing knavery of a passing world on holiday.
Approaching, in the wavy heat, he can see a figure, a brown man,
Thick, bald, skittish, sweating slightly in the sun,
Turning behind at intervals, hopelessly conned
By the illusion of knowing that he cannot catch what is not there,
And that what is not there cannot catch him although
This something behind is snapping at his ass, like furies.
And Johnson simply looks down as the other approaches,
Watching his soft, soft, black shoes shuffle hurriedly;
But he does not see the creased, crisp trousers,
The gorgeous silk shirt, open at the throat, billowing,
Flaming red, carelessly framing with elan the history
Of the hard, huge shoulders of the last hero of the free world,
Who held within his blank eyes the only small virtue of his clime.
As he sits roughly at the white covered breakfast table, unseeing,
The Malacca cane clatters down; the cat starts and bristles;
And he mutters over and over again the single word: zero.
"Come," says Johnson sweetly, tough prince of the demimonde,
Smiling and thinking, *poor fool, believing in his disbelief*,
Tossing a section of tangerine, nodding, his eyes as thick as a
  wizard's,
"Let us eat and enjoy the breakfast of champions."

The Autobiographies of Ex-Colored Men, Part II

(for Tiger Flowers, known as the Georgia Deacon because of his meek, religious demeanor; the first black middleweight champion, circa 1926, who died while undergoing a minor operation for the removal of nasal scar tissue; an operation identical to this killed his white nemesis, Harry Greb, a year earlier)

Blessed be the Lord my strength, which teacheth my hands to war, and my fingers to fight . . .
— Psalms 144:1

I.

How is the reading of the sacred text in the home
Of a Georgia Negro, gathered before the clan, stopped?
The sconces go out, the living room is darkened, outside
Eight white men stand upon a lawn in white moonlight, pale themselves.
The stars come out quickly, a blank holy range of light, stopped in heaven.
"Come out, friend," a white man calls to the dark walls of the dark house.

He emerges, an old cave savage in shawl, out upon the lawn in the light,
Turning his back, keeps turning his head back to the house and the darkness,
Catching the creak of leather boots, steaming breath, the headlights of trucks;
My God! he thinks, My Dear God, it is cold out here; my chest is cold.
"Kin I go and get ma coat?"; he rubs his shoulder, pulls his shawl, no one answers.
"Do you like to beat white men?" asks a voice in the ring. "Do you?"
Not unfriendly, a curious voice, a question like "Nice weather?" or "How's missus?"
But he doesn't answer, saying, "It's a cold night for you gent'mens to be out."

II.

Before him, shirtless in the cold, pale, stood the big white boy:
"Jem want to know what's it like to git hit by a prizefighter."

The pink-pale chest bare to the cold, a broad belt, leather boots, a cough:

"It's a cold night, Mista Jem. Lonesome. Ain't you cold and lonesome, sorta?"

White men stand in a circle, steaming breath, headlights, whippoorwill, no eyes:

"Jem want to know how hard a prizefighter kin hit; if one kin break his jaw."

By the sixth punch to his face, the shawl falls, flutters like a dark wing:

"Jem want to know if them fights is real life or if they's fixed like real life."

He missed every punch he threw as the white boy bloodied his nose in the cold:

"Why, your time is way off, friend. Must be the cold air. Night air ain't good."

III.

How he wished he could lie in the frozen mud forever, hard, in the darkness.

Hands, two or three or more helped him, brushed his back, picked up the shawl.

In the light, he could feel the steaming breath muss his hair; no eyes; men without eyes.

Turning, he heard a cough, "Good, friend," and did not thank God for forbearing.

The Autobiographies of Ex-Colored Men, Part III

(for Sugar Ray Robinson, great middleweight and welterweight champion, who suffered from Alzheimer's disease)

(for Muhammad Ali, great heavyweight champion, who suffers from Parkinson's disease)

> *I have made my bed in the darkness.*
> — Job 17:13

       Conceit:
Corinthian-like it stood upon his cool brow.
How grace abounding mingled in that dark skin,
Reveling hideously in its patient wait for lightning
In the eroding masque of the milling prize ring,
The flash that smote, blasphemous, arising from deviltry itself,
The sharp black eyes, the well-cut clothes of aerial fancy,
The conked, smoothed hair of midnight, the style of menacing sin.

How now he sits upon a wicker chair, in the early evening,
And in the soft darkness, soft and bloated himself, unshaven,
Sluggish as a thick worm, coiled and coiled upon itself,
His eyes dulled and shaded by an utter and sweet night,
So silken in its descent to seem almost a noble, hard-earned peace.
He smiles a boyish smile, aged devil, and turns calmly, waiting for
    the moon.

In his youth, trench coat open, collar up,
He walked across the bridge from a stalled car,
Out in the light, striding across the lines,
The cooing birds above his head; a progress
Unlike any other; colors and light in one, color and light,
The tangled skeins of an hour of flaring awe unstopped,
Signalled by the crumpled paper in his strong brown hands;
The audacious coming, it was, unleashed, of insouciant salvation.
O how the knowing coves stood before their Lucifer unbounded;
Unblinded, amazed, in remembrance of that blooded figure
Of poetic war that could be loosed with such appalling élan
From that beautiful and touching body of love.

Satyagraha

> *(for black British middleweight Randy Turpin who, years after beating Sugar Ray Robinson, shot his youngest child and blew his own brains out)*

He coughed, as if he had a heavy cold, spitting,
A hard cough, as he fell across the room, bumping
His head against the bird's cage and, swallowing

Phlegm, opened the cage door to let the nothing
That was inside out, and then he lurched backward,
As if he had no legs at all, to the bed where a baby slept.

He sat on the edge of the bed and stared around
At the room, felt his sour tongue touch his teeth,
His strong yellow arms between his knees like a boy,

And was hardly surprised that nothing in him could
Be touched by wonder or boredom, madness or a rage
That would have made madness approach the richness

Of an infinitely rich art. But there was no rage
For there was nothing to remember, for rage to know,
Except that he had once been, he knew, a strong man.

But now nothing to know, not even the glory of standing
In the center of the circle of yellow light, yellow arms
Upraised like a light hollowed from a more savage light;

Drunken money spent drunkenly by a drunken man, the
Odor of a woman's belly on his lips. The nothingness
Did not even know the wild whiteness of the white city,

His blanched smile at the brass band that played
For him there; only the black vomit on his shoes seemed
Real as he coughed again. Blankly, he stooped and kissed the

Sleeping child, bloodlessly, like a ghost drained even of
His ghostliness, and looking through the window could see clearly
A cricket match, the white flannels, the batsmen, and such a

Long delicious motion of the bowler. How he wished such a motion
For himself! He walked to the center of the room, posed, his arms
Ramrod straight, his face as resigned as a useless prayer uselessly

Uttered, for one last time watching the bowler run forward, a boy
Really, and a motion so much like an orphan's missile to the sun.
And then turning, awaiting, with the supremest gift of wrought

Patience, the last gift of the strong man; and with that, turning
As if suddenly struck by a dreadful ringing in the ears, thoughtfully,
He was bathed by a white noise as stunning as the white streets of
   heaven.

Soon, One Morning: The Last Stand of Andy Bowen

> *Andy Bowen was believed to have been a black lightweight from New Orleans who participated in the longest fight conducted under Marquis of Queensberry rules. That fight took place in 1893 against Jack Burke and lasted seven hours and nineteen minutes, or 110 rounds. Bowen died the following year, at the age of twenty-seven, as a result of injuries sustained in another fight in New Orleans. His race remains a mystery, as it was impossible to tell whether he was black or white.*

There was this sound like running milk,
Thick and white, cascading
On the ground in splashes, mixing
With the dirt and turning dirty itself.
He thought it was like a kind of fallen light, falling
From some secret height in his mind, a failing light. Out,
Out it was. Out it was like that. But it was not light at all,
Just something like light: a running stream of milk,
Flowing in a wave like the arm of Buddy Bolden in a white suit,
An arm waving to a crowd, a blurred arm, milky and rich
And running like white paint wet upon a picture or a fence.
He had fallen so quickly, dropped, that he was blinded by the white milk,
As if weakness were to be the only and final testament of his strength.
Beyond his fingers he sensed the bruised fruit upon the ground, pulpy things.
Blood popped from his ears, forming bubbles on his neck: more milk,
He thought, all the milk in me coming out, falling from my fallen self.
And when someone over him called his name, he opened his eyes, astonished,
Betraying the rapture of seeing savannahs, the glowing milk of beatitude
Running like some endless sap over some endless land.
Such looking, he thought in his last thought, such looking,
I must get up again to get hit again to fall again to have the vision;
While the others stood over him, amazed completely by the wise eyes of the dead.

Part Three

The Art of the Chest

Tribute to the Art of the Chest

(for Jo Jones and Philly Joe Jones)

If therefore thine eye be single, thy whole body shall be full of light.
— Matthew 6:22

Some people are standing there, in the act of witnessing,
In that gloom even though it is raining and
Even though it is only afternoon and is still raining;
There are some who are compelled to witness a tiny spectacle,
A mere speck of haunting force in the larger storming;
As the rain falls and the afternoon, of course, grows darker,
It is a good time to bear witness to that conceited strength, hideous
In its source of that which is so dreadful but is truly virtue after all,
The only virtue we may witness: the drummer practicing his
   drumming,
His back curved and his face a blank kingdom of other faces
Awaiting the surging of the conceited strength, the thumping in the
   chest,
To make a single face of the image of the tiny spectacle of what our
   faces mean.

A downward *swish* of cloth on a dancing dancer! The thudding *thud*
   of the dropping
Of the great weight! The crackling *crack* of gates standing aside for
   kings of glory!

He flips his sticks and raises his head to smile suddenly, in virtue,
Aglow in the darkness, wet with wonder, to let us know who are
   standing there
Witnessing while it is raining that there is more light, great fist in
   the chest,
More light than ever we have ever dreamt of.

Old Dirt Road

(for Jackie Robinson)

Turbulency,
A wave of clatter, impossible soundings,
The murmurs of tongues gathered in this place,
Our consensus of the tangled blood of our character,
Resounding to the dark stuttering of his tongue,
Waiting to bat on a windy day, the high, white sun,
The billowing white uniform against his black skin,
The billowing flag, the spangled anthem, arising, too,
Too like a turbulence, a miracle of storm, a stupendous,
Unthinking courage, a force realizing itself,
A gale running the bases as if to outrun all the
Running that ever was run to some other place,
Canada, perhaps, or running on the wetness of the sea,
Or in remembrance of other fields, dirt roads, scorched cotton,
The billowing possibilities of a sheer, unthinking freedom —
There, upon this field, muscular and black, a disturbance,
A face, black and boyish, that wears the burning and burnt triumph
That shapes forever what our unutterable unhappiness is.

Ulysses As the King of Spades

(for Bill "Bojangles" Robinson)

Not on his knees, he would not;
The ground was cold, his trousers
As sharp as anything cloth that
Could be creased and so, his silk
Coat open, colored and aglowed by the sun,
He would not get on his knees to
Throw the dice but rather, on his
Haunches, flung his hand, opened his
Fingers in a gesture of such beauty
As to think this a dry, dark dance,
A step of such color as to deny any
Limpid whiteness as a partner in its
Magic that could only finally say that
If sex is not all, then it is a kind of
Everything in the energy it could waste
In such a daring, useless, laughing flick as that.

He picked up his winnings, grinning, straight
And lean, his silk coat open and showing a
Golden-handled gun that seemed a sign of someone
Who wanted a peace that only warring could bring.
Turning, he walked away, effortlessly jumped
And clicked his heels, one-two-three,
Tossed the money to the ground behind him,
Winked at the street lamp and beheld the men
Scramble for the loot with his special
Knowledge of what tales could be told if
The street corner could say the anything but
That the world is the everything you make of it.

Chief Crazy Horse Meets Caliban

> *For you know, nuncle,*
> *The hedge-sparrow fed the cuckoo so long*
> *That it's had it head bit off by it young.*
> *So out went the candle, and we were left darkling.*
> — The Fool in Shakespeare's *King Lear*
>
> *To the just-pausing Genius we remit*
> *Our worn-out life, and are — what we have been.*
> — Matthew Arnold's "The Scholar Gipsy"

Bud Powell peered down the stairs as Bird was coming up, a dark figure,
In darkness, puffing and puffed, his feet flattened in soft slippers,
His face wincing in the darkness; he had a hard way of it:
Up, swollen eyes bland as doe's eyes, while Powell laughed, giggled; up
He came slowly, clutching a saxophone like a golden serpent
Hissing in his hand, writhing like a captured beast; he looked
For all the world like he would not, could not, walk again, ever, not another step;
He looked like someone who would not make it up, who would just sit, at last,
A sloppy, drunken man who is laughed at by Bud Powell, a crazy, sober man,
His finger pointing: "Old man," he called down, "Old wineskin in the smoke.
Where is, jive man, your confidence? What do your idylls mean? Burning genius,
Where is thy great genius now? Old pig guts. Cocksucking wineskin in the smoke."
And so gently, gently in the mockest love, Powell blew him a kiss.
But up grunted the old, fat, drunken man, sputtering and cursing,
Feeling that his pain was that by which other pains were made
To cease being pain but simply the common art of complaint of ordinary life.
And when he reached the top step, face to face with Powell, near the ledge,
Watching the light over his shoulder, Bird held open his palm,
And for one moment he seemed to hold the biggest, brightest bouquet
Of flowers that ever was, a blinding thing of colors, nearly hideous,
Its sharp petals bloody in his hand. And then he spoke in Powell's ear

Secretly like a secret agent: "When sound sleep falls on men, while
They slumber in their beds, white sheep, then he opens the ears of
　men:
Herding happily to the instinct of knowing without knowing what
　their idols mean."
And dropped into Powell's a smooth, sweaty series of rocks, no
　flowers,
That smelled for all the world like actual bullshit, really so they did,
And pushed him aside, and walking in pain like some wounded
　bear,
His nose pointed toward the light of the bandstand by which he could
　make his way,
He emerged, hobbling yet grateful, once more from the whirling
　cave.

Bobby Timmons' Live Soulful Jazz

The master of soul jazz is not
The master of himself tonight, though, of course,
To be thus divided is something that
He has, in the fullness of his buxom
Imagination, learned hard to live with;
Being beside himself, sitting at the piano
And wondering, amidst the gathering of ice,
Lying, the chatter of getting laid, clatter,
While sitting there, where else, in God's
Name, he could possibly be sitting now

In addition to being here and not wanting
To be all the while there, some other where
Also. His cinnamon eyes scan a buxom crowd
That too wants to be nothing but itself but
Wants everything else in order to be nothing,

Nothing else at all. He sits at the piano,
And someone asks him if he were not this,
The master of soul jazz, what on earth would
He be? And he says not on earth but jumping
Away on a bucking horse or rampaging steer

At the moment, when being a bronco buster,
Cowboy-booted and perched like a whim upon
The black, hairy back of an unstoppable buffalo,
Jerked in the air, outstretched before the horned
Sun, as an unknowable a thing as anything can
Possibly be in this wholly unbuxom world.
His cinnamon eyes lash downward to the keyboard
As if he wished it were something in him that
Would go of itself without him, unstoppably gallant.
His dark and curly head falls forward as if garlanded
With plaited palms and blue-veined petals as he begins
To play soul jazz, as if anyone cared, that is quite
Beside himself again with a fervor that is, surprisingly,
Like a ringing jest, as if he cared, that is quite beside the point.

The Fire-Eater, or the Engaged Artist As Miracle Monger

(for black magician Presto Johnson)

"Fire-eating," he said, "is a cold art,"
As his tattooed arm quivered, his belly
Creased and groaned; his splintered laugh, parted
Teeth, his ruined black tongue, like a spoiled jelly,
Licked the flames, cooed the smoke, coughed sparks.
Like a dying star he was, the child was sure.
In the fire-eater's dressing room, a dark
Devil he was turned to a white star, a lure.

The child was sure of that, a sellout, false.
Everything sold for white stardom, not winning the
Fire anymore but a giving of freak pulses
To a jaded crowd, a child's game of pinning
The tail on the dragon: be a sort of make-believe viper.
"But water," stuttered the child, "k-k-kills the fire piper."
So the fire-eater mulls and muses with a quiet ire,
Then mutters, "Nothing can kill fire but fire."

Amagideon, or When Lee Andrews and the Hearts Sang Only for Me

1. "All that pass by . . ."

In the lunar year of Tet,
The white and gold mummers strut past my street
Hard-eyed as Endicott, gorgeous as the daughter of Jerusalem,
On their way to glory and the house of glory;
Cold in the iron arrow of wind they are and coldly, coldly
They play the hot music of sin as no one listens
But everyone stares and thinks
About some dear old southland of the mind:
A large meadow where peasants sing hauntingly,
A square where girls wear kerchieves and dance by themselves,
A deep well where tired men drink clear water.
The mummers do not smile at anyone;
They are simply passing through on their way to another country;
They are visitors who, in passing, know the way out.
No one smiles at them in their plumed splendor,
So much like the clergy of a Reformed church at holiday,
So much like Calvinists gone to carnality,
So much like the dazzling armored conquerors of a strange land.
It is, alas, just another dream of pillage,
A fantasy of serene and easy plunder
As a train of sleepwalkers in morning raiment
Are caught still in the refulgent fury of the winter sun
In a forgotten place where people do not
Like the hot songs of innocence
Played in the iron arrow of cold wind, unmoved and unmoving.

2. ". . . clap their hands at thee."

On this plain, where the carnage
Is denied its feast of bells and prayer,
And where the eye is full of
The landscape of scandal and chances;

On this plain, where there
Are no trees, no sky, no billowing swell,
No grazing animals, no book
That reminds one of the myth of experience;

On this street corner as broad
As a broad, equivocal sea
And as hard and blank
As a wall built to hold back that sea,

There appear the ghosts of five black boys
Who have just walked and strolled
As coolroot and coolloving in
Florsheim soft, soft shoes
Down and down the pavement project stairwell,
Sequined, hair dewed and done and damply cocked,
Zootthroated shirts and gold teeth aflame,
Gonads aflame like a cosmos.

They sing in Chaldee,
High-pitched as Vishnu, the disobedient god,
As if there were no misery but the mere lilting sadness
Of homesickness and homelessness
And the final hope of a more final wisdom,
Singing as sad as Curtis Mayfield or Smokey Robinson,
Clyde McPhatter or Johnny Ace or some other
Drowning sentimental man, eyes thickly filmed
Over and over by requests to battered women to forgive them,
By requests for one great song sung in blessing,
And always knowing that nothing in this world is requited
But the very things that one does not want
Or things that one does not deserve to have — it is unfair and
   goodnight.

In the world of pederasty, cops with smoking batons,
Magical agonies of lust and dust, mojos, dead fucks,
Babies sailing into night, Coke and lye concoctions
For unfaithful lovers and lying friends,
Only paunchy hustlers with wounded prostates,
Only raunchy old girls with bad teeth
Remember when Sonny Til and Billy Stewart sang
On the corner the cool songs of experience
And remember that it was a time of moving and being moved.

There, on the street corner called
Diamond, Tioga, Gray's Ferry, Dauphin,
Where pigeons swoop like mad darts,
Where hieroglyphic walls decay
In the refulgent fury of the summersun,
Five black boys sing a solo song around
The campfire in gathering evening,
A vast song that can be heard across the widest prairie:
The old, sweet song of the range.

Stairway to the Stars

(for Bill "Bojangles" Robinson, known for dancing on stairs)

His shoes were like chrome, shone like
Polished chrome, as wearily he waited in
The wings for some act to be finished, a
Dog act, then something with flight, doves
Flung gracefully from a scarf, red and
White. He could scarcely breathe, as
If the entire theatre, the whole world itself,
Could not contain air enough for him,
Annoyed by a loose button, a frayed edge
Of cloth and realizing while waiting there
That he was finally a scarred, old man,
Wheezing, wizened, weathered, weakened,
Not chrome like the shoes but as worn
As floors upon which his feet had stepped
When, in his weariness, his mind had slept:
Coming upon the stage with a smile that
Was not bidden but brought forth by a
Man who seemed bitten on his butt by
Some abiding demon who, unbidden, would
Not let him rest or break except by bits.
An odd light, creamy, enriches the glamorous
Shoes of a colored man who dances entrapped
By the pressure of an unbending cinematography
While offering the lumbering tap, bow and bend,
Of an awfully bruised Tyrannosaurus rex, a
Cowed cattle, doomed, from the dim, dangerous past.

Innocency, or Not Song X

(for jazz pianist Bud Powell)

Remember, I pray thee, who ever perished, being innocent?
— Job 4:7

It was not warm,
        not what he thought, not warm
But cool, dirty, dirty
        and cool, this very small space
Under the car, there,
        under, where he thought it would be warm.
A space, before he
        went under, down under, thought to be a yonder
That was yearning for
        him, for which he yearned himself, a calling;
To be under the car,
        the grit, the oil, the dark, cool metal mazed,
A sort of breathing
        thing, not breathing, as if one were buried,
Buried in the belly
        of a calm machine, under and away, sheltered.

The high, white moon, which
        he could remember sometime ago, a shape of light,
Sometime ago, in his cell,
        amply detained as mad, he could remember through
The mesh wiring, through
        it, the high, white moon, there, circular, oracular,
A center of something
        not held, staring blankly, calmly back, as if
It were the expression
        of some impossibly contained oneness of fellowship
Like being alone in
        the church upon the hill called home, sweet home of the
            Lord.
He could see it even
        when lying on the floor, straining up, staring,
His face sopping wet from
        the water they threw on him, icy water on a bitter night,
The bucket of dirty, icy water
        to awaken him from dreaming the oddest thing:
*

In the cell, in the light
       of the moon, stood mocking the light, stood before him,
A huge rooster, almost monstrous,
       nearly three feet high, white and black and red, spangled,
An erect thing that did not,
       absolutely did not move and that did not seem as if it
          could
But which loudly, loudly
       crew enough to shake the walls, out against the white
          moon;
And so he thought himself
       the powerful cock, bedazzled, chanting, erectly, not song x.

He lay beneath the car,
       his face sopping with blood, escaping the police,
Absolutely not wanting
       to face the high, white moon anymore ever,
Only wishing forever to
       stay mad and safe and small and hidden and down.
The face of his one
       last friend peered down, soft white, a moon of sorts:
"Please," he said, as if
       it were a prayer to a boyishly sweet, starry god.
"Please," he said, bending down,
       and the other looked up, crumpled, as if a child,
So small from beneath the
       car, as if it were that heavy thing that, shielding light,
Stopped a thing so light,
       so utterly untouched, from being a kind of aerial wonder;
His shoe touched the
       puddled gutter; his sleeve dragged the grease;
His face, beneath, under,
       could not be seen, only the buried voice, soft, grave,
With so much quivering
       that his friend could not imagine, even signifying yore,
That from that prostrate
       figure, that prostrate state, could come a humming
          utterance
So dazed, fallen, so innocent
       that, at its saddest, it could not possibly be any song at all.

D.W. Griffith's Picture in the Papers, or Room for Romance

> *Yet it is true that most wealthy persons lead the most prosaic and uninteresting lives, whereas the doings of our friends in denim and calico are aswarm with the most amazing romances and tragedies and dramas of every kind.*
> — D.W. Griffith, in 1919, when *A Romance of Happy Valley* was released

It was his stalking across the cutting floor,
So announcing the presence of his absent attention,
Rapt in contemplation about the shapes of swords and viols,
A still life so voluptuous that he could,
In utter amazement, clinch his teeth in regret
That he had after all only mere women to frame
In fields and rooms, haunted by dark seductions, whose cruelty
Could only be enormous tributes to an exquisite need for sin.
And this made him think himself stalking across the floor,
Tailored in Bond Street clothes, with coils of film at his feet,
Curled and crunchy like cockroaches,
While he, southern cubist, thinks of himself thinking,
Thinking what to say to Lillian Gish
In a scene as if she were there and he were carrying
Pails of warm beer home, as his father might, that is,
As if he were her father, carrying home pails of yellow, oily, cheap beer
And she, at the window, seeing him, then coming out, crying "Papa,"
And he holding the pails, one in each hand, the sun setting behind,
The country warm in color and in corn, a green world,
The green heart of the greenhorn in a green-gushing, ordinary world;
And he holds his pails and hopes that she, small she,
The beautiful child of cunning concupiscence, ripe simplicity,
Would say romantically and softly against the soft, green hills,
Would say, "Gold" and would see the pails of warm beer and cry "Gold" again.
But in this scene, she runs up and peers at the pails of warm beer
Only to turn away and cry "Piss," and again, louder, "Piss."
And those with him on the cutting floor flinch and glare
As they watch him, thinking they see him sitting
Thigh deep in his cut, curly film pieces, staring ahead,
When, of course, only he knows that he has poured out
The beer, unable to touch his star, and soils
His beautifully tailored trousers by sitting in it.

Specific Jazz, or How Birdland Got Its Name

By the window goes a street
That is called "The Night
Has a Thousand Eyes," that
No one, I mean no one, can
Understand how a street is
Called "The Night Has
A Thousand Eyes," except everyone
Knows it is the place where we can imagine
And sometimes even hear someone
Named Charlie Parker suffer
An aggrieved sottishness in
The rot of a white hospital, white tile,
White towels, where, in some ward, one knows
About the soft, rising panic of his fat face,
About the pudgy boy whaled, wailing, and walled
Between blankness and the moment of art becoming
Art, and there he is all straitjacketed,
Imagining himself, in his mind, I mean,
As something like an oxcart pulling up the sun
While he sits at a table in a club called the Peru Club,
Or a club on Peru Street or a club really in Peru,
His saxophone against the wall, all aglitter,
As he buys drugs from someone who can,
Of course, on a good night, talk
About something like the social history
Of the epistemology of the poetry
Of Wallace Stevens or the life of Bessie Smith,
Which is always the counterpoint
For the tale he tells of himself
Of the burning of the fire
In front of his dew-covered eyes,
That is not himself or
Any part of anything of himself
But some otherness that burns,
That he has always known to be there
And for which he has alternately pouted
And entered women in the hope of
The fire, sort of, you know, playing,
I mean, playing itself out so as to
Not be there now while he imagines
In someone else's imagination who
Is imagining that he is looking up
*

From a chair at an attendant, whose
Whiteness, blocking the view of a
Moonlit chapel, is the only single
Whiteness in all that darkness,
Like the gentlest snow of morning.
And looking up and out and away,
He repeats, "Flanders Fields" and
Repeats, "It's Flanders Fields again."

Lawrence Talbot: King of the B-Movies

(for Lon Chaney, Jr.)

Imagine the difficulty of waking up
Without shoes on the dark, cold moors, the howling sound,
The rain in a mist, the wet, lank hair, the hot, white face like
The light that kills the moon that kills the civilized,
Waking to face the silly gypsies, a fair, rich girl, a bungled life.

Imagine the difficulty of remembering
Another vaudeville script, the set made of occasional paper,
The unfooled children at matinees, the drunken director, miscasting,
The minstrel makeup that simply makes a beastly nigger of you,
    Beat
Ravisher madly buckling up the bungled absurdity, the bungled
    nothing.

Imagine the difficulty of escaping
To skitter across the wet, sharp rocks, the dogs in pursuit,
To slither into the damp, lightless caves, to stamp across marshes,
O Princes of Faces! The lone howl, acrylic, like an atonal
    notation
Acknowledging the sleep that lies in the bungled habitations of the
    mask.

The Dreadful Bop of Flyers

Part I: If You Could See Me Now

(for Tadd Dameron and Bud Powell)

There is such that's in the mind
That loves the slaughter: the walking
Through the shambles of spirit, the bone
Spotted with blood, the ragged reggae (they say) of watching,
Pressed small against the faceless sky. Ah, here (they say)
The flyer soars and plummets like a burning thing,
Aflame and ghastly, a light streaking madly to its end of light:
For the flyer can fly only while falling
And can be light by not stopping the falling,
A twisted, twisting lighthouse brightening
The perishing edges, the decaying circles of the landscape.

There is something in the eye
That matches the slaughter and the story
Of the slaughter, that is (they say) this, no other:
In his flight, the flyer might think of one still life —
To think of one porcelain cup,
Thin as a wafer, white, polished and filled
To its brim with strong, red tea,
That (they say) is made from leaves and berries.
The cup is still, its liquid still,
In a still room, where the wooden table is made gold by sunlight,
Uncluttered by junk, occasional wood: the trinkets of small minds.

Bunyan and Wordsworth lie open, leaves unruffled and stiff,
And the walls are cool and smooth like the marble walls
Of a church without junk, which is (they say) the
Slaughtering adornments of restless minds. And in the room,
Against the background of nothingness, one can hear
The sound of a spinning jenny, a tw-tw-twirling tinkering;
Strong fingers quietly guide the skein.
And the flyer is probably reminded in his flight,
As the ground rushes like a mad terrazzo to meet him;
And the flyer is surprised by, in his mirroring mind,
The occasional sublime peacefulness
Of the Great American whir of Pietism,
When the mind and the eye are not engaged in slaughter.

Part II: One O'Clock Jump

(for Count Basie)

. . . When my foot slippeth, they magnify themselves.
— Psalms 38:16

Once upon a time,
In the time of slaughter,
In the shine time,
This is how the poor
Spent an evening in Jersey:

"Their foot shall slide in *due* time,
For the day of their calamity is at hand,"
Said the woman, lit with God and sweat and crying.
The boy, fingering occasional wood, could only think
Of the Amazing King of Jazz and his Water Babies,
Who made him recall the chant of loons on a placid lake.
The boy had heard him play, the band of shine time, seen
In his mind the whores, trailing like houris, kissing
With love each dusty Edwin Clapp step, each sliding foot,
The stickpin diamond, the throbbing elegance.
And the boy thought of parachutes in the wind,
Full and billowing, bright and colorful,
Speckled with slaughter they were, like balloons
Touched by clouds of misty, misty, foamy blood.
The boy knew that only parachutes saved one from the fall,
That they rescued — like lusty men and women parts,
Umbrellas, ladders, plants, and the light in darkness —
By opening up and out and taut.

"When I said, 'My foot slippeth,'
Thy mercy, O Lord, held her up,"
Said the woman burdened by slaughter, lit by God.
In the shining, smiling moon, the boy,
Touching occasional wood, played for saints and thought of sinners,
The Amazing King of Jazz and the laughing and
The playing and the dancing women or just the
Dancing legs of dancing women, which shall
Slide and slide in time while dancing skirts
Open up and out and taut before the Amazing King of Jazz.

Part III: The International Sweethearts of Rhythm

Coming through bitter weather bitterly,
It was nearly Christmas, a cold Christmas,
And, she thought, this is no way to spend Christmas,
To spend Christmas at fifteen, lugging, lurching
With a battered tuba, cold fingers on the cold case.
At fifteen, she thought, how nice to spend a
Christmas opening a box of cashmere sweaters,
One after another they would tumble out; cashmere —
A rich word that sounded like another she heard, Kashmir,
In a newspaper, on the radio, from a teacher, someone.
To pull cashmere sweaters from a box on Christmas,
One after another, all the colors rainbowing out
Like flares of light against the warm Christmas sun
That would seep through the window, touch the tinsel.
Not this at fifteen, she thought, a broken-down bus,
Nearly Christmas, and coming through the bitter weather
With fifteen other girls, lugging a tuba case:
Stupid, ugly instrument, stupid instrument for cows.
She stopped and found herself in a wide, wide meadow.
The others, heads down, were farther ahead, and so
She stood alone, covered with a fine white, like ashes.
Her eyelashes were white. Her eyebrows were white.
Her stockings were soaked. Her fingers were cold.
She felt, for a moment, like an ash-covered cow, a stupid thing.
She dropped the tuba in the field and began to walk away,
Toward the others far ahead, without her tuba, head down.
After walking a bit, she turned and saw a blackbird, you know,
Those winter blackbirds sitting on the tuba in the fields.
She could see the blackbird through the bitter weather,
Through the fine, fine white that covered like fine ashes.
I am only fifteen, she thought as she ran back, sliding and
Slipping, losing her feet in the wet/whiteness; I am only
Fifteen and not meant to spend Christmas like this, carrying
A cow instrument like a cow, falling like a fool in this field.
She ran so hard back to the tuba that she fell entirely and
Smashed her lips against the case, hard against the black case.
Her fingers touched her lips, touched a wetness, unsure of blood.
She sat sprawled in the whiteness, her shoe off, her coat open;
Ah, just to stay here in the bitter weather, and think of Kashmir,
*

To think of cashmere in a box at Christmas, the colors of cashmere.
Up she is in a moment; her shoe is broken, so she puts it in her
    pocket.
Up she hoists the tuba, and, walking unevenly, down and up, she
    goes
(Calling her fall the dreadful plop of triers, the dreadful drop of
    hiders),
Through the bitter weather, thinking it a long walk, through the
    whiteness,
Through the ashes, at fifteen, to the gorgeous gift boxes of colored
    cashmere.

Country or Western Music

(for tenor saxophonist John Coltrane)

What I say is, for Christ's sake, you don't
have to kill yourself to swing.
— Count Basie

He could not imagine himself a hero at all
Of anything, remotely, standing there
Playing a long solo on the saxophone.
He could not imagine his playing heroic;
He could not see himself drawn in an epic;
He could only see all that dark-blue darkness,
And the playing was not the light but merely
The request, in nakedness next to nothing,
For some smaller luminosity or some less darkness.

He thought of his saxophone as a confidence man,
Coiled and golden, like a goose of surprise,
Who offers him a choice between a glass vase
And any seven words ever uttered in the language.

The vase, for instance, is sitting on the table,
A glass vase, thick, pure, and clean, with
A body that suggests circles that are not circles
But the roundness of the something of a circle
Or an ellipsis or a parabola, a coin, a bell curve,
So, a glass vase sits, fat as a viol, upon the table.

It could be one thing or another to the eye,
Broken or whole, containing white flowers or black marbles,
Sitting on the edge of something or the center,
Gilded or bare, trembling or still, water or air or earth within.

But how words, up and out, lead to heaven.
The seven words shimmer, a dazzling throttling up
Of possibilities or the consumption of artifacts.
How we ache for voracious discourse, the princely imagination
Of fire at the end, desire, the metaphor as the ghost in the belly.

But it was not *that* that he wanted, not to beguile,
Not to be beguiled by vases within or words up.
He did not want a human sound, a human meaning.
He did not want a human song, only warmth and movement,
An idyll burnished like metal by the inhuman guttural gold of
   himself.
*

It is not the great solo, not the song of songs,
But merely the cry of indifference, the quaver of solitude,
The eyes of the forsaken casted up, the arms dangling down.
It is the only and the most remote love he knows that we can ever
 know.
And so of course his solos are unfinished, incomplete, beginnings,
Because the only way to con the confidence man is to keep him
Waiting for the ending he expects until he, like you,
Expects no ending at all.

The Lonesome Death of Sam Cooke

He could not believe his own blood spurting,
Gushing like a virile jet of vermilion spending itself,
That some woman had shot him in the belly,
His flat belly, like the surface of a table, erupting absurdly
And spewing life all over himself like a baby's spittle
Or as if he had so much life to give as to tend to wasting.
He wanted to get up, to move toward a whiteness that hurt his eyes,
Which was only a brilliant sort of acid extinguishing in his mind,
His heart, enlarged and whitening weakly yielding to twilight,
To catch that whiteness in his quick, hot hands, so much
Like a kind of cold burning on his brow, like a sulphur.
But he could not move anymore, even in his mind, could not catch
  anything.
He could only sit in his own excessively bright blood on a lustful bed
In a squalid, squalid room in the unreality of some vast, fat sin
Growing thicker and blanker and mute as his body ebbed to zero.
He touched his face with his red, glowing hands, smearing himself
Like his ancestors, frowning, smeared with color, a warmth.
It was so much in him that he wanted to sing for his Lord,
And now, in the end, unable to sing, to speak, to sigh, only
To wait for his life to stop flowing out of him so he could think.
His red hands he thrust forward, holding out in appeal or prayer or
  anger,
As if to welcome some infinitely savage angel from a savage,
  infinitely dark god,
Realizing, despite the white sulfur, that he was just some filthy
  pagan after all.

A Ghost Writer's Song in Remembrance of Romance

(for Billie Holiday)

> *. . . and the laws they live under,*
> *seem to them weapons of romance.*
> — Emerson's "The Poet"

> *Romance is mush . . .*
> — Billy Strayhorn's "Lush Life"

1. The Lyric As the King of Culture

Asleep,
Asleep in a rainstorm,
A scudding shower of fleecy foam
(Though the rain it raineth every day),
Sheets and sheets of rain, fierce and heavy,
Water rich as light, dense as light,
Twisting in the light of street lamps,
Humming like viols sawed by savage hands
In a jungle bearing a savage profile and toppled stone altars.
It is, this rainstorm, as if
One's fate were a mixture of several seductions,
Small cans of frozen orange juice, a new piano coolly wooden,
A green car always out of gear,
And old music on the radio where the DJs
Are forever talking and selling things,
Aging tomorrow before it is even tomorrow.
She once sang in a rainstorm
The texts of cheap romances, bore
A canary on her shoulder, wore
Shoes of thin, crisp leather, the earrings of summer; there
The gallant whore of stardust
Let fall a flapping sheet of music to the ground.
It was the last time that she was the girl,
The heart's desire of our real dreams,
The courtesan, formal and miraculous, staring
Out of the cafeteria into the rain.
It was the ambiguities of words that frightened her,
The interpretations of lies, the beguiling hazards of poetry,
The critique of passion without passion's blood.
We wanted to luxuriate in crafted lusts,
Voluptuous voyeurism, the rhapsodic Zen of bellied prophets.
*

At last, at last she knew that what
We wanted really was not feeling
But the morality of feeling, not
Drama, not art, but melodramatic lures
Told as romance over and over again, forever.
The rain had been the only sound we had ever loved:
The woman in the rain — the last totem of the western world.
And then, realizing that, at that odd moment,
She suddenly discovered that she could not sing anymore.

2. The Lyric As the Memory of Romance

Asleep in the unmasking of thine own night,
Asleep in a room nobody knows,
The quiet clock has lost time,
Now a minute, now another,
Like the horological drips of a leaking faucet,
Chronometric cracks in an unplastered wall.
The room is too small, too tiny,
To hold even two small mink coats,
A hairless dog curled in the corner,
One hundred hairbrushes,
Three dozen half-used tubes of lipstick, and
Bottles of lotion, creams, scents, soaps, mouthwashes,
An original Madame C.J. Walker Hot Comb,
Makeup for scandalous eyes,
Scandalous lips, thick as rind,
Muttering: "But Bird ain't alive.
Bird is dead. Chippie Hill is dead. Ma Rainey is dead."
And we muttering back: "What living
And buried speech is always vibrating here . . .
"What howls restrained by decorum?"
(She was a patriotic girl:
Make the boys happy for the war effort.
She wanted to make them happy, rascals and knights,
But who wants a painted woman's slow drag for customers
To spot the unsullied flag of honor,
Of redemptive light and heralded gore?
Patriarchs fight only for honor, the rebellious glory,
Death as the cunning ordeal of righteous wrath. Bird lives!
And she did not want to sell war bonds dressed as a maid.)
The television is on, always on
*

(Tonight she saw Elvis Presley
On another Frankie Lymon on still another
Lena Horne singing a Bessie Smith song,
Then Louis Armstrong performing a coon ditty
Written by Hoagy Carmichael as a lark,
And a girl group in wigs:
"You say you gonna meet me . . .
Tonight's the night."),
But the screen is blank like a wall, a blank buzz.
She wanted two things as a child:
A snowman beyond the window of her room,
To watch it melt in the sun,
To have the drips of water dazzle in her hair,
The gallant virgin in the sunlight,
And she wished a pure kiss from her mother,
Peaked with tenderness, filled with sweetness
Of young children singing in gold-glittered voices
On the gutted street sheeted in fog as white as water,
As white as pure light; there
She remembered the children singing (in her mother's kiss)
"If I could, I surely would
Stand on the rock where Moses stood."
It was the first gardenia she ever saw.

3. The Lyric As Several Passages from an Eastern Autobiography

Other children sang songs that she could remember.
In plain dress, the Catholic girls sang
In plainsong at Christmas "The Holly and the Ivy."
It reminded her of dirty bedsheets,
The Confessions of Augustine unread and unopened,
And the symbolic piety of girls on their periods.
Then there were six tall girls in the back of the whorehouse:
"I'm leaving with my baby, don'cha know?
I'm leaving with my baby, don'cha know?
Now, the night is soft and my lips are, too;
My baby is a man who can really do the do.
So, I'm leaving with my baby, don'cha know."
The whorehouse was filled with curving rooms,
Fine-hammered wrought-iron staircases,
Incense, drowsy lights, women with curved backs,
*

Lacquered tables filled with volumes of studies on Sufism.
She stood before the mirror, mesmerized by her body in a slip,
Black stocking tossed against the lampshade, singing:
"If shadows get up and walk around
And willows that weep began to sing,
I wouldn't raise my eyes."
The other girls chatted away, sitting on the bed,
Smiling, drinking pop, as if they were daughters in a Puritan family.

4. The Lyric As the Subversive Sense of Ending

In this room, the bedsheets are dirty;
The goldfish bowl is dirty;
The fish swim and die in a murkier season;
Minimal gore flecks her plump arms,
Which matches the refulgent gore of her hair, her nails,
The small canary that chirps on her shoulder,
The innocently witnessed carnage that scandalized her mind.
She once sang in a voice as broad as a Byzantine organ.
She does not remember that voice anymore.
She dreams of the deific enterprise which
Has always been, shortly put,
To outlast the longest, longest love by one year.
It is too late to learn this another way,
The lesson she taught to Hazel Scott,
Realizing another blues statement at last.
It is too trite for words.
It is so trite that only words can serve it; these words,
Some short stories, are all there are for the last romance:
"Autumn in New York," it's good to live it again, or
"The Kingdom of God" is within you.

The Staff Writer's Quest for an Historical Yardbird

> *No vital force comes into the figure unless a man breathes into it all the hate or all the love which he is capable.*
> — Albert Schweitzer's *The Quest of the Historical Jesus*

I sit on my bed in the late and declining evening.
I know it is evening because on the plastic radio
I can hear four or five boys singing something lonesome
About "I only have eyes for you," and I am dreaming

About a story of hagiography I will write while
I sit on my bed in the late, declining evening,
Knowing it is evening because on the plastic radio
I can hear four or five boys singing something lonesome

About four or five boys playing something very cool in what
I dream about: a story of hagiography I will write while
I sit on my bed in the late and declining evening,
Knowing it is evening because on the plastic radio

I am listening to a song called "Charlie Parker on Tenor Sax,"
Which is about four or five boys playing something very cool in what
I dream about: a story of hagiography I will write while
I sit on my bed in the late and declining evening, absolutely

Ready never to move from the soft, white warmth or to bear the crossings
To invent the song I am listening to called "Charlie Parker on Tenor Sax,"
Which is about four or five boys playing something very cool in what
I dream about: a story of hagiography I will write while I sit.

Four Songs at the End of Winter

(for Thelonious Monk)

a. Rhythm-a-Ning

"Professing themselves to be wise, men become fools,"
Said Armand, the scowling owl, instructing his friend in school.
Tar the cat, bored, was in no mood to be taught.
"Hand me down my walking stick. There're marvels to be sought."
So saying, Tar the cat, cane in hand, hat on head, begged his leave.
But Armand the owl, holding him back, looked entirely peeved.
"You people," spoke the owl, "petty gods, always wish to play
And look upon the serious ones as jive, out-of-step ofays.
Knowledge is not experience gained by mere living and being
Unless everyone be wise and every heart an instrument of seeing.
Knowledge is a hard-fought thing disengaged from riotous feeling;
It is not the gift of mere play performed on stage as a rite of healing,
No laying on of hands, no unconstructed sounding of sensation;
For every act of art by method generates a like act of explication.
Is improvisation of the moment really better than written work?
Or is the altar of mental discipline where only the foolish lurk?
And you have changed the glory of God into the image of
   corruptible man,
A crawling, creeping beastly thing, not essence but spit, air, and
   sand.
Yes, my feline friend, there are attending marvels in this life
But not open to the eye of nature but to the symbolic eye of strife."
Armand, now silent, profiled against the moon, let fall from his
   claw
Battered copies of Dante, Fielding, Johnson, and works on man's
   great flaw.
Tar the cat waved his cane like a wand across the beautiful, dark
   sky.
"I am not so learned as thee, my friend, nor can match eloquence so
   high.
All the world wears the mask; 'tis playing of some mystic game
That is more enjoyed when played than thought about. I make this
   claim:
That everything that lives is holy and there are not truths not seen;
The world is a mask, a label, and to participate is to mean.
I know naught but life, for life begats life and so does death fling
All dead things back into life, so everything that lives is Swing.
In Paris, Richard Wright and James Baldwin do bloody battle,
*

But because I am a good timer does not mean I am simply driven
   cattle.
Now I must go where my ideas and style of life will fit,
No puritanical correspondence, just folks talking that signifying
   shit."
So saying, Tar the cat, his wand now a clarinet, rides on,
While Armand, the scowling owl, moves from the edge and waits
   for dawn.

b. Misterioso

Miles Davis, soloing, an impersonal angel,
Considers the posing of possibilities
Of several sets of table manners
For a meal that consists of
The disemboweling of wolves
And the immense eyes of ostriches
On a tablecloth of small, blood-cut circles.
In a club called "Desolate Heaven,"
He plays his last set, no codas,
No requests, and stalks off the stage
In a cloakish cloud of Spanish leather.
When asked to play a tribute to Monk,
He brusquely says, "Fuck Thessalonians."

c. Think of One

A blonde girl combs John Coltrane's hair.
He sits on his bed, a saxophone in his hand;
A thin line of spit connects his bottom lip
To the tip of the saxophone's mouthpiece.
His eyes look very sleepy. He cannot keep himself awake.
Red Garland chides him gently from the corner of the room.
"What the hell you call that? A ninety-minute solo on a Monk tune?
Where is the blues, man? Where is the swing? What you call that?"
Trane looks up, his eyes thick with dreams:
"It's ninety variations on the goddam ambiguities," he says.

d. 'Round Midnight

Imagine some austere figure,
With blue spats, laced, elegant gloves,
Coughing and dancing
Slowly and more slowly in the coldest air,
Making blood-cut circles
On the soft, drifting snow,
Announcing the late
Arrival of spring.

Swing to the Many

(a tale of Louis Armstrong and his valet)

It was the everyday notion of it, the lack of newness,
The familiar movement etched so rich in wornness, plushlike,
That pleased so deeply his sublimity of spirit as he laid
Out the clothes as though they were priestly garments

Of a man who could, on favored days, broad as the sun,
Long as moonlight, be seen as a dumpy Lord of Hosts,
Be thought so devoutly so, a stout, brown Grace awkwardly
Come to the table, a rotund and fickle divinity, laughing.

And as he laid the silver trumpet there with the rest,
He turned as Pops walked in, head-ragged and robed, tired,
Plopping as he sat and stared and sat and frowned and sat
And wondered at the thing, this trumpet, that had, through

Him, brought such sweet swing to the many who knew, a lightning
Wire glowed and gone. O, what we pay for fire! Looking, he did,
As if disgusted with how shallow only happiness could be, as if
He were casting about for another room, a spare room in which to

Know his perfectly polished pitch of pain, to suppress the cry
Within, a cry beyond any scale he knew. He coughed, spit, lit
A cigarette, gazed unsmilingly at his clothes, the silver trumpet,
As if their arrangement there was a boredom he could not fix or
    place.

Lost, he looked, rubbing his cheek, to think it comes to this:
This sitting, this room, these clothes, the man who lays them out.
And so his valet touchingly looked at Pops as if in some exquisite
    gratitude
But only to say, "Sir?" as if that soft utterance of servitude, of
Rendering up to please, would be like applause ringing in his
    master's ears.

Diet of Worms

> *Men want women pink, helpless, and do[ing] a lot of deep breathing.*
> — Jayne Mansfield

On this given Sunday morning, bright and gauzy,
Bessie Smith wears a peignoir of plumes, her hair
A rain of ends and knots, dreadnaughts, as unruly looking
A black bitch as anything seen near a stage since

Topsy, as evil and uncivil as that, a fat, black Topsy.
And she waits, Bessie Smith does, for a breakfast more
Sensual than the previous night, for what can be more
Erotic than eggs, sausage, glasses of beer, chocolates?

Then, flouncing through the door, comes Ma Rainey, oiled
And slick, arranged in a mink coat as glossy white as the
World's white weather, who sits at Bessie Smith's vanity,
Smears her gold teeth with vaseline and turns her fat back

To the mirror, legs cocked wide like someone mounting a viol,
And considers herself a sight for sore eyes in a white world
Of white gaunt love, an uncivil world answered only by the
Incivility of blackness and fatness, jelly-rolled elegance,

A reign of vulgarity. Ah, Topsy's downfall was her diet after all.
Too thin she was, and gaunt, not fat enough to grunt, to specify
That it does not do for a black woman to wear her poverty of
Unloveliness, gaunt and white, like a certain class of catarrh,
   leprous.

So is the lesson of Topsy, the last, gaunt, unloved queen of the
American stage, who existed in dread for our sore eyes only,
   blinding.
And so, in remembrance of starvation, two fat black women,
   American
Mammies, blues singers, if you will, sit eating and drinking, civilly,
Plumes and white mink, explicit coiffures, regal poses for a flawed
   kingdom.

James Baldwin at the Apollo Theater, 1968

It was, he knew, this singer's shout, like a sound
Of ice beaking in an icy bowl, a chilling reverb, a
Crude resonance like the sea tumbling in a thimble:
Call it singing, which is like singing in a certain sphere,
Where the sound of singing is nothing more than the
Raising of one's voice in protest against the cracking
Of ice on a hard surface, the sea gorging the globe.
As he twisted in his chair, his tie askew, wanting to smoke,

A blues song sung by Sam and Dave could be, he knew,
An ancient mummery, a moan captured in a glass of light,
A strange smiting upon a spiritual chest, which made his
Own voice rise within against the multiple deceptions
Of his words' own uttering fury, a taut, taunting reverberating bow
Protestingly inept, which reminds others that "You Don't Know
   Like I Know."

Part Four

Consensus Vessels

I believe in Love.
— from "Throwing a Good Love Away,"
Phillippé Wynne of The Spinners

Consensus Vessels

(for Ida)

In October, she, in her formal, white suit, rests
Her arms lightly on the sill to watch
The growing darkness of the sky, to hear
The wet sound of damp leaves on the ground,
And suddenly, quite suddenly, to wonder with wide eyes
At the waving, white patch and the little girl
Across the yard with braided hair,
Dressed in a green school uniform,
Who looks at the dark sky with wide eyes,
Who wonders, while listening to leaves wet in the wind,
At the woman whose arms rest lightly on the sill.
So she waves her handkerchief, her school emblem, fluttering
Like a big, silly flake of snow in the darkening air
To catch the woman's eye before the deeper darkness comes.
And the woman, who can barely see the girl
In this obscure light, sees enough
To recognize a sister lover of autumn,
An eater of apples, a climber of trees,
A scatterer of leaves.
Together, she thinks them to be the sweet heroines
Of some sweeter novel and, in some special secrecy,
When the lamp quiets the anarchy of mind,
In a sacred moment of convergence of eye, through darkness,
Meeting eye, the suited woman and the Catholic girl,
Two sassy sojourners, can imagine themselves
Sailing down a placid stream to a golden house,
Large as a lighthouse, ornate as a mosque,
Where other pilgrims gather and tell tales
Of nothing in particular about the convergence of things.
Or she thinks of them, uniformed girl and Protestant woman,
Working like two shy servants in a garden of stubborn weeds.
The woman strikes her hoe against the thorny ground,
Sweating and hoeing, and the girl stops, quite suddenly,
And disappears and, like a sprite, reappears,
Running, bringing to the woman a glass of cold water,
While, overhead, some birds, dark in the sunlight,
Converge with the sky. But it is almost too dark to see,
And the woman, feeling the end,
Wants to acknowledge the girl,
*

To acknowledge the accident and wonder of convergence.
So she waves her white handkerchief too, across the yard,
Fluttering two big, silly flakes of snow,
Both together saying hello and goodbye.

The Art of Chess

*(on watching Linnet and Rosalind play
chess, and what I learned from that)*

The symmetry of order is not stopped, the
Lushness of the Lordly mind from which comes
The Rule of having rules, a refulgent discipline
That tells the where and how to move, the sweet
Logic of plotting, the finality of strategic grace, victorious:
Ah, to be saved solely by the reason for being saved.

The symmetry of order is, too, bounded, captured,
Undone by the capers of capricious minds, bowling
Children unbowed by Rule, untasking discipline, colored
Chess pieces bowled across a board, abroad, in the air,
In the childish air, pieces of movement, scattered,
Smallish women plotting without moving there, bowling over,
The final ends of reason or the reasons for what we reason, or
Contemplating on the floor, two uneasy pieces, queens of Misrule.

Grooveyard

(for my mother and father)

> *Past three o'clock*
> *And a cold frosty morning*
> *Past three o'clock*
> *Good morrow masters all.*
> — Victorian Christmas carol

Later that same morning on Christmas Eve, my mother is all alone,
Not with anyone else, not even me, alone, except herself,
And this record by Johnny Ace, scratched and old,
That she remembers first hearing at the Bedouin Hotel.

It was there she heard it in the ballroom or the basement,
As a dancer or maid that she heard Johnny Ace singing
Something like "forever my darling," like he sings on the record
That she is playing in that room, a small room, in her house.

She is not sitting in her favorite chair or any easy chair;
She does not think there is any anything like easy sitting when
She is listening to Johnny Ace on a record or in person
Because that is the time to stand in the center of the room.

And she does not weed the garden like other mothers and
Grandmothers in poetry, who work with tools and look from
　　windows.
She is simply alone, inside, no view, because it is cold outside,
Because it is Christmas Eve, because there is nothing whatsoever to
　　look at.

She does not like the cold outside; she stands in a heated room
That is like the heated room where she stood on some other
Christmas Eve, coming from the Bedouin Hotel hearing Johnny
　　Ace
With some man in uniform, smelling like a fragrance as blank as
　　water,
A fragrance that filled the room on Summit Avenue where they
　　lived,
Where she could smoke in bed and he would sit on the window sill,
Where, for the black eye he gave her one Christmas Eve, half-
　　smiling,
He placed a red, round ornament in her hand and placed her foot
　　upon his head,

A fragrance as dull as any fragrance sold in a drug store

With prophylactics, with gum, with a newspaper, with ice cream.
It was not the touching of his greased hair out of duty, out of love,
That mattered. It was only having heard Johnny Ace in the ballroom or

Basement of the Bedouin Hotel; only that mattered, and the standing now
In a room in a house without an easy chair, alone, on some other
Christmas Eve, when there are no handsome men in uniform like swift, rampant princes
And one can afford, as is richly joked by some, to love and to be loved in return.

Occasional Rain

*(for Coy Oglesby, my late stepfather, a police officer
and the first man I ever saw wear a gun)*

Something like this happens when the barber first cuts your hair,
Or when your mother cuts your hair and out comes your cap,
Or when it snows and you don't expect it, cut by the ice, or not,
Or when you find some money or when you don't but you'd like to,
Or when your singing sounds very good or when you know it
 doesn't,
Or when you expect the world to end but it keeps going and so, drat,
And so do you keep going and wondering why it all doesn't stop.
Something like this happens in the fullness of knowledge
That comes in spying suddenly a man's strength so hidden by
His weakness that it seems a wonder in the knowing and in the
Dunce-recognition that you can never know anything —
Yourself in himself or that weakness that is the weakness of
Your strength and the clear appreciation of the modesty of
 manhood,
A not-muchness that is a habitable wonder for its puny insight,
A habitable light, small, but which held your mother up, and up,
And too late to tell him so, to tell him how you liked his good
 speech,
His not-so-good goodness, his good eye with a gun, his
 understanding
Of the helplessness in others that made his helplessness such
 wisdom,
Such a habitable wonder that, in its modesty, only few men can
 attain,
That, only that, the something like a will, not whim, that joins
 momentarily
Against something like the fate that cannot be changed, nor charged.
And something like this happens when it rains sometimes.
 Sometimes
Something like this, near enough to this, like this and only this,
 happens.

Why Isn't Marseille Said the Way It Looks?

(for my youngest daughter, Rosalind)

Sitting in the center, more or less, of
Her room, surrounded on either side
By dolls, black and white, plastic and
Cloth, naked and clothed; by books, some
Picture, some all prose, a very used copy
Of *Trumpet of the Swan* tented out on its edge
So precariously as if it dare not collapse;
By dirty sneakers, scuffed "Sunday" shoes, and
Six different "hand-me-down" dresses from
Her big sister's closet that, as she says,
"Ought to go back to big sister or to the poor
Because little sister does not like them";
By pages of piano music that refuse to be practiced;
By a half-scribbled notebook with copy from
The encyclopedia for tomorrow's book report;

She eyes herself in a hand-held mirror, smiling
Just so, smiling as if pleased as punch by some
Prettier-then-thou image of a little girl swinging
Her just-pressed hair to and fro as if this small gest
Pantomimes an answer to the question of why
Things are the way they sound instead of how they look;
This waif, kiddingly cunning, who, in her eye's corner,
When seeing someone watching, is inclined by a
Generosity that not even she suspects she has
To grant forgiveness as a small, careless gift pulled
From the largess of her abundant stocks of glory.

Pragmatism, or Jehovah's Witnessing

(for my uncle, a Jehovah's Witness)

*But watch thou in all things, endure afflictions, do the
work of an evangelist, make full proof of thy ministry.*
— 2 Timothy 4:5

I'll take nimble steps.
— Shaker hymn

He had, unknowingly, walked straight
And smashed his head against a tree, saw
Stars in daylight, and suddenly, as if
A tree had grown from nowhere and in God's
Wisdom was meant to strike him unwittingly
Or he it, hard enough to have half his wits
Dashed, and suddenly, blood gushed from his
Bruised nose, and he thought God had a hard
Way to show, after all, that real is real
And so to humble a voluptuous mind to its
Own carnality as stunning as the carnal
Earth, the carnal sea, the carnal air.
He could not breathe because his nose was filled
With blood and his head filled with stars
As he stumbled to a door and rang the bell and
Felt his trousers for a handkerchief of any size
And thought, while wanting water, that he
Must remember why he was knocking at this door,
That he must tell whoever opened it that this
Was an at-home that he or she knows not yet is
His or hers, that today is the day for your
At-home though, of course, you don't know you
Were chosen for the at-home where all the kings
Of glory shall come in, attending, beckoned and
Beckoning. He shakes his head as a woman with
Bonnie blue eyes answers the door, and he holds
His head up, and his bloody nose drips upon his
Shirt, and *Watchtower*s and *Awake*s fall from his
Fingers, and stars befuddle his eyes, he thinks,
Like some enchanted evening, and all she sees
With Bonnie-blue eyes is a bloodied black man
Who says dementedly, although he thinks he is
Asking for some water or remembering how children
Teased him as a child with, "Your nose got to run,
Your head gets rubbed," but is saying, "Praise God
*

For gladness," and so she says, "Oh!" startled, and shuts
The door, and he, startled too, swoons to the sumptuous
Feeling of strangeness that comes with earning the difficult
Knowledge that organizing God's at-homes require.

The Cure

(for Linnet)

Touching the part in the middle of her hair,
It felt to him for all the world like an etching,
A severe tracing with a pencil, such as her face with tears
Was traced as he lifted it up; autotelic, he thought, as if unhappiness
Were, for him, after all, only an art form, like wearing one's hair.
Change your hairstyle and you're no longer unhappy, he thought childishly.
As she there, seated at her unfinished game of jacks, the small ball tumbled down,
Metal stars flung across the floor like so many awkward auroras.
And so he said, "Let's make spaghetti tonight together and eat in."
Moving around the kitchen, its worn floor, the father diced onions, found an old garlic;
The girl rinsed tomatoes, cut the green pepper, found spices in the back of a pantry.
She gathered the water in an old pot, and he tied an apron 'round his waist,
Covered the girl's hair with a kerchief so she looked, for all the world,
Like his sister, when, as a child, he watched her tie kerchiefs 'round her head.
And boyishly he told bad jokes like: "When is a door not a door?"
"When it's a jar, Daddy," the girl said, impatiently but smiling all the same.
It had not occurred to either the man or the girl that perhaps
This is the way praying is or that the answer to praying is, alas,
Prayer, a prayer for our praying to which we must listen
To know that the answer to our prayers is the act of praying
For an answer to them, not on our knees, but on the kitchen floor, worn as it is,
As the man and the girl, unknowingly, glided by each other, lightly,
In step, making the meal as a rhythm, together, a couple arraigned
With divine ordinariness as if it were, this kitchen, the starlight of a ballroom,
As if all magic were just the doing of what must be done by someone
And as if all unhappiness were absolved by thinking how we, such sociable saints,
Mustn't step upon each other's toes in the doing of our simple chores,

In knowledge that our dancing is the gracious sum of one and one,
  our sum of grace.
(Ah, stardust on the kitchen floor, as we, in that light, count the
  steps to reach our own height.)
And they, father and child, the last couple, in answer to their prayer,
  for that one evening's
Short but stately chorus, richly danced with graceful industry onto a
  beam of eternity.

Thurifer

(memories of St. Mary's, an all-black Episcopal church)

He is so startled by the sight that he
Almost loses the step of the cadence,
Stumbles, as if sand were in his eyes,

So to seem to others there that he falters
In some graceless, boyish way; charming,
They might think, as they think he thinks

Of baseball or the brown eyes and brown hair
Of some brown girl borne back upon him like
A rutting, hot memory: cuddly concupiscence,

The scents of hot puppies; but what is is not so, not
The warm Devil's valley makes him reel like an

Earthling made blind not by the light which he expects
But by too much darkness. *Suppose*, he thinks, *suppose*.
Such a lot of rubbish to put one's faith in, to hope

That the world is not some great one's rubbish heap in the end!
And you no finer thing for having hoped. Lord, Lord!
Why should the world be more than the Lordship of Orlando

Cepeda's brown arms or the thick, soft, smelly moss of thighs
To rub our faces in and say no one's the worse for the rubbing?

How could God be contained in such a silly vessel as we,
Like children, made from sand and sky, without a clue, cueless,

Going *olly, olly, oxen free* in a hide-and-seek game?

So, his head bowed, he picks up the step again and steps
In time, brown yet grave, with his eyes unfocused ahead,

So that others, following in step, do not know the infirmity
Of being a boy touring without a Baedecker, scattering the fog.

Some Memories of an American Girlhood

He was, for me, standing there,
A prince of the sublime, black and evil,
Waiting for me, just waiting.
And me all of fifteen, fresh
And fine and looking for trouble,
Thinking, if sex was everything and
. . . if looks could kill, if gestures mean . . .
And him standing in the doorway
With that cherry-red, opened-up car,
Standing there for me in a sky-blue suit,
Curly, black hair, black autumn eyes,
Fast hands and nasty, nasty eyes, black skin,
A thin, long cut on his cheek and chin,
A woman's wound, luminous and angry.
Such a nasty look he had, like the most delectable king of kings,
With a smooth, garish, glowing guitar around his neck, hanging
    there.
"Wanna go for a ride, little church girl?" and his
Absolutely foul mouth sounded like a sort of
Euphonious fathom sounding deeply on my inner ear, smart and
    lewd,
Spitting between his gold teeth, fast and nasty,
And looking like the kind of excitement
That only a good dose of sinning is bound to bring.
And me thinking, maybe I won't, maybe I won't,
But saying, "I always have been a bit skeptical
Of the evidence of things unseen, if you please."
So then again, maybe I did. And so on and so on.

Dumbo's Ears, or How We Begin

(for Linnet, my daughter)

there is always talk among the knowing kind
if you are last to do a certain thing or anything or everything

>that you are a slow one, as slow as the time
>it takes to say anything twice or more

>that you helplessly do not see the plainest
>sights to be seen anywhere by anybody plainly

>that you are as ungainly as Dumbo's ears, as
>clumsy as a childish elephant with floppy ears,

>but there's always been a kind of pleasure
>in a certain kind of slowness like a gait

>that sort of ambles a bit through the park
>or shuffles along the street, sort of stopping

>and not quite knowing where it's going, because
>what with stones and leaves and silver rabbits

>and silken insects and all manner of infinite trash
>and voices and echoes and signs and the wide sky,

>well who could help but be subverted in one's quickness
>if one is really a sky lover and likes to watch the earth, too.

>so there is no real reason to go anywhere in particular
>except the somewhere that anywhere can lead easily

>along some way or other until another more
>outright way comes, a way that is more a gift

>that would make the gait even slower and more stately
>like a meandering stream's or a balloon ascent

>or a blues saxophone's or the words of a wedding or
>the reading of any text worth the wait or water

>evaporating in a glass — all a kind of awful slowness
>that seems, like our gait together, to say *wait awhile*

and which, like the whiling tortoise, always starts the race
after the quick and the hares, gate open, in their blind rush, begin.

Listening to Frank Sinatra

As a boy, when you entered the tent,
Darkened and wet like your childhood,
You kept straining to see around or
Through the adults who were there;

You thought it smelled worse than any
Place you'd been before, and so you strained
Not to smell, and you strained to see as
They paraded out. A sorry lot they were, too:

A grossly fat woman, a man with scaly skin,
Someone with a body like a tube, someone
With an appetite for glass and nails, and,
Last, a man with a bag over his head, a

Plain, brown, ordinary bag that everyone,
Waiting in hope, thought concealed behind
The horror of horrors, the most grotesque
Of the grotesque; he was your star that day.

With one sharp intake of breath, the shudder
Of utter joy that you were not, at last, this
Junk heap, we saw his face and wondered, *this*?!
And as he told his story, someone asked, jokingly,

"What do you do all day?" and he said, smiling,
"Why, listen to Frank Sinatra," as if *that* was,
As if everyone should or would do what was the
Most natural thing in the whole, wide, natural world,

Reclining somewhere after work to listen
To "At Long Last Love," or "You Make Me Feel
So Young," or something else that helps
Get you through another day of just living.

And then, you thought later, what could he know
Of Frank Sinatra, of sitting with a girl in a
Darkened room, kissing wet kisses, driving
Along a dark, wet road, with the hum of the radio.

But when you left the filthy tent that day,
It was all you could remember, all you thought
Of, even after you forgot the face of horrors:
Listening to Frank Sinatra gets you through a day.

Ahhhh, such a story I like to tell my children
When we go out to tents and shows and sideshows
And I keep straining to hear Frank Sinatra off
Somewhere on a PA or someone's radio and they,

My children, always staring, wondering why
Their father is the crazy one who wants to
Hear Frank Sinatra where there is no Frank Sinatra,
Where no one else wants to hear Frank Sinatra at all,

To which looks I reply that if Frank Sinatra could
Do so much for the man who was the horror of horrors,
To sing such that he could make it through a day,
Just think what such listening can do for me.

Destry Rides Again

(for my childhood friend, Destry, the first and only "cowboy" I ever knew)

There is a certain affrighted look that only,
In retrospect, I realized, a city black boy could wear
Out in the snow, his hand held aloft, his fingers
Webbed with flakes, his battered sneakers wet, weary
From busting broncos, standing between the trolley tracks, his
  cowboy
Hat tilted, o bronze-skin buckaroo, with a dare upon his lips
That only those who understood nothing in life but fear could bear,
Could, pressed and plucky against the cold, witness without wonder.

"Come on," he said, "we're goin' out west to sell these shopping
  bags."
And out across the stores we went, the scout and I, hawking our
  wares, braced
Tightly against the range wind by the fire that only fear and cold
  could spark.
"Bang! Bang! You're dead!" he'd laughed, pointing a deadly finger,
  smiling,
And I, slouched with homage, imagined us both magically watched
  by rodeo angels,
Ahorsed, the cowboy hat receding, the scout leading, a nuanced
  rider, across the prairies.

Five Études and a Jeremiad

> . . . *for long periods he would stand looking out, at his pale window behind the screen, upon the dead brick wall.*
> — Herman Melville's "Bartleby, the Scrivener: A Story of Wall Street"

I.

Not knowing, on my birthday long ago, my mother gave me,
Sealed with a dark, hot kiss, a white album, a tradition,
Which now I open, on another birthday, for my daughters,
Who as one start and blink, for when opened, the white album
Reveals white, rough, blank pages, stiff and blank and fibered,
Veined like the hand of the old or the wings of a butterfly,
And from them fall a fine white dust onto my lap,
My chair, my green cup, my dark books, my scores of grandeur
Scattered here and there about the floor; all over it falls,
Swarming like a kind of sand, a powder that fills the nose like scent,
Like the alabaster glory of the blond, tenacious light.

II.

One day, my daughters and I, with basket,
Went forth in the country to picnic,
And with us we took the white album, out into nature,
And spread its leaves upon the blanket, the white leaves,
While, in a distant tree, haloed in the setting sunlight,
Several dark, awakened birds watched us, waiting.

III.

The thick, green cup, filled, sits perched nicely
On the white album on the window sill,
As I lie in bed, tired, worn, heavy with eating,
The counterpane rolled away, something speaking, looking out;
My daughters play in another room in a darkened house
A game of clasping and releasing in the round,
Then, surprised, say, "Who? Who's there?"
Or is it I who says that who, that who's that there,
At the sound of the radio in my room, a talking horn?

IV.

I grease each of my daughter's knotty hair, black hair,
Knotty and enfolding like Medusa's, tangling my arms;
My fingers rub with heavy blots of heavy bergamot,
*

Scented with roses, enriched with lanolin, thick, oily,
While they hum a bit, perched between my knees,
With parting of the hair, the wonderful smell swelling up.
The water faucet drips brokenly in the sink
Against the green, thick cup, thick green, a love's sound.
With guileless eyes, dense as Ormazd, my daughters,
Whizzing with the sound of accomplishment, with their box of
    Crayolas,
Stroke, line, scribble, and fill a white page of the white album:
It is the crackling and dragging of some alien voices to me.
With greasy hands, I seize the white album, the Crayolas,
And it and they are soiled like the sea is soiled, like nature is.

V.

I stand at the window, the white window of a white life of eyes,
White eyes of life, there, standing at the window, looking,
In the autumn, the red, dry leaves of a red, dry autumn
Everywhere, and my daughters playing there, in the red, dry leaves.
Then suddenly stopping to look at me, looking up at me and
Pretending not to see and pretending I do not see,
They remove from one jacket the white album,
Bury it like they do in the red, dry leaves, and from
Another jacket comes the match with its red, dry light:
Yes, Cordelia and Goneril setting fire to red, dry leaves and a book
Of whiteness, witnessing the burning of the whiteness
Of the white album, the three of us, knowing in the
Red-hot fire is the delight of the doing of the undoing of
Some ancient, alien text, crumbled like a great white wall.
And there, rising, only the burnt scent, the thin smoke,
So hazy in the red, dry autumn air as to seem to us
Like a rising leviathan of some other light.

With Ida at the Pacific Ocean

There is the god that has transited away,
Leaving behind only this beach of dirty sand, this salty air,
These salty seas of infinitude, a sunset like a wound
To remind us of the bloodline of being made flesh and dwelling,
In some sweep, forgotten in its majestic robes,
Fallen or tossed away, a remembrance of an uncurling, conceited
   presence
Of some galloping god streaking across a universe
That will not end, a racing child or racing horse
Unsubdued, leaving only this vastness from its pockets
To remind us how alone we are with each other only for loving and
   raging
And these excessively wasteful objects of the excessively fertile
   god:
This beach, this air, this sea, and the standing upon it with another,
Standing and staring, in loving austerity and blank opulence,
Feeling a fumbling, rough wonder at being left so far behind.

With Linnet and Rosalind at the Pacific Ocean

It comes back again to you,
Not the blank, insistent wave,
The broken vanity of the burnt-over beach,
The high-pitched, mongrel cry of gulls
Like the lyricism of loneliness, cracked echo;

The immensity returns, the wasteful glory
That overruns and overwhelms the eye,
God's boyish scrim, a magical show,
All light and more light, silken and stark,
All stair and star, all space and sand,
Like some miracle, breaking and spiraling,
Like some grand toys strewn about the void,
Like girlish laughter filling a morning,
Dim-voiced verses bunched and splintered,
As two children run along the shore
Chasing a boyish God, a promised horizon, the tender
Hope and mercy of a perfectly tempered tomorrow.

Teaching Contemporary African-American Literature

At the end of the semester, when the surveys wearily
And winding go modern or postmodern, as you will,
Comes upon you, in the big anthology, something by
Amiri Baraka called "A Poem for Willie Best," then
Someone asks, "Who is Willie Best?" like an echo
From your own child who, watching some old Charlie
Chan or Shirley Temple movie, asks who's that silly black man there,
Which is precisely a question you asked your mother

In a dark theater long ago. In 1962, you heard someone
Behind you say he died at 45, penniless, in a relief home,
Completely alone, holding an autographed picture of Sugar Ray
Robinson as if it could talk to him, as if pictures could talk, easing his cancers.
In the silence, someone asks are he and Stepin Fetchit the same.
In the darkness, your mother answered, "Willie Best is just another name."

Lear and His Daughter

In the house you live in at the end of the street,
In the darkened room there you can think about
The fly crawling on the television screen, serene,
Or you can think about the light that drew it there,

The light of the set, the rented film in the VCR,
In the lateness of the hour while you sort of doze,
While you sit watching, your head falling forward,
You can think about this blond girl on a sexual jag

Right before your eyes, which have seen everything anyway.
You can think about the girl, young, supple, moist, open,
And how much she seems like your eldest daughter,
How the resemblance startles and annoys like pinpricks,

How much she is there like your eldest daughter might be,
How she might break your heart that way by doing this.
As you sit and watch a group of men surround the writhing girl,
Hearing in the background Billie Holiday singing "Everytime We
   Say Goodbye,"

You think how much irony is not a pun but a certain heartbreak.
Of course, you can think about the something you've always wished
As far back as childhood, when you wanted to be the emperor of
   everything
And when you could think that being the emperor of everything

Would mean that the seizing of any random piece of ass
Would really be like what the song says, a "Stairway to the Stars,"
And that every casual gesture of lip, tongue, buttock, eye
Would not be wayward gone to heartbreak, just acting, but
   something like

"The Nearness of You," "Dedicated to You," "You'd Be So Nice to
   Come Home To."
Dozing, watching several men at the same time fall upon the blond
   girl,
You do not care about the men, and the blond girl does not matter
   anymore;
Your eyes have seen everything forbidden, o mystical voyeur —
   hark! and

The wishes of childhood will not turn a thankless child to gratitude,
   make
*

A piece of snatched ass anything other; sitting and watching does
   not
Make heartbreak any other than the wish that one did not really see
So much, so much misery, which does not make you think of mercy
   or
Any benighted blankness or anything other than the ineluctable
   expressions
Of heartbreak within the realms of heartbreak, the horror of
   nothing to express
With no expression at all; only acting after all, that you may think
   of while
You sit and watch in a darkened room the rented film in the VCR
   and the fly
That is attracted to the screen which, in the darkness, is the only
   light there is.

With Linnet and Rosalind at the Mouth of the Mississippi

Think of the topicality of water,
Floods, the generation of possibilities,
The reaches of karma muddied on the banks,
As two girls with far-flung hair, framed by starlings,
Brown as Buddha, gazing upon the lastness of the river
Sun-glazed, polluted, a long stench drifting.

Think of the topicality of blood,
Insects starlings eat, the possibilities of generation,
The river some oily, plotted road, a pollution,
As two girls, brown as Brahma, with far-flung hair,
Consider the discomfort of sharing a room with their father;
Moody with menses they sit, still, luminous as stone.

Lighter Than Air

(for Ellen Raben, my Catholic friend, and Dorothy Day, my Catholic teacher)

> *Those waitest for the spark from heaven! and we*
> *Light half-believers of our casual creeds . . .*
> *Who hesitate and falter life away . . .*
> — Matthew Arnold, "The Scholar Gipsy"

At night, in that cold air, the snow, a-flutter, a-float, flakes seed-like,
Seems to curve and bend as some slow, burdening
White creature, like an ox, bright and blind in the darkness,
And blinded herself, the driver shudders, her shoulders
Hunched, her fingers grasping the wheel, her ear dumbly
Attuned to the sound of the darkness, the sound of the
Curved, bent snow, ox-like, being blown whitely in the cold air
And to all the nothing that is the snow, the air, the car,
This moment of driving, herself, the nothing within and without,
Just the sheer boredom and desperation of getting home, at night,
As if a home were, after all, the effort of numbly getting there,
Driving, oxen-like, a driven, heavy obedience, blunted, weighted like freight,
As if, guided by some blank omniscience, a colder governance for a cold world.
But what if for one moment her ear is startled by some other sound,
A plumbing, radiant depth within the great code that to this earth, this
Water, answers silently the great code of all outside the progenitive heart,
The everything that is signified in all the nothing that is there, outside,
And seed-like, perhaps, she feels herself rise, bursting, bubbling oxen, a-flutter, a-float,
Lighter than air, streaking by everything she knew, every home, all unreal as all she thinks she knows,
Enchanted now like Christ, a dazzling mystery, her hair full of snow and darkness,
Her breath white, like lithium, torching the night, scorching the cold, combustible air,
Chanting the fierce prayer of how fierce and unstoppable love is, dear, holy refulgence,
A-flame like the divine racer, o liquid, speeding church, that God used to so torque the world.

Sussex Carol

That we, too, bear, under this illusive edifice, living stones,
And the breaking, in aching splendor, of our willful bones.

Biographical Note

Gerald Early was born in Philadelphia, Pennsylvania, in 1952. He graduated from the University of Pennsylvania and received his Ph.D. in English and American Literature from Cornell in 1982. He is currently Professor of English and Director of the African and Afro-American Studies Program at Washington University in St. Louis. In 1988, his collection of essays, *Tuxedo Junction*, was awarded the $25,000 Giles Whiting Writer's Prize. His essays have appeared in *The Best American Essays* series in 1986 and 1991. *How the War in the Streets is Won* is his first book of poems.

Also available from **Time Being Books**®

LOUIS DANIEL BRODSKY
    You Can't Go Back, Exactly
    The Thorough Earth
    Four and Twenty Blackbirds Soaring
    Mississippi Vistas: Volume One of *A Mississippi Trilogy*
    Falling from Heaven: Holocaust Poems of a Jew and a Gentile
        (with William Heyen)
    Forever, for Now: Poems for a Later Love
    Mistress Mississippi: Volume Three of *A Mississippi Trilogy*
    A Gleam in the Eye: Poems for a First Baby
    Gestapo Crows: Holocaust Poems
    The Capital Café: Poems of Redneck, U.S.A.
    Disappearing in Mississippi Latitudes: Volume Two of
        A Mississippi Trilogy

HARRY JAMES CARGAS (Editor)
    Telling the Tale: A Tribute to Elie Wiesel on the Occasion of
        His 65th Birthday — Essays, Reflections, and Poems

ROBERT HAMBLIN
    From the Ground Up: Poems of One Southerner's Passage to
        Adulthood

WILLIAM HEYEN
    Falling from Heaven: Holocaust Poems of a Jew and a Gentile
        (with Louis Daniel Brodsky)
    Erika: Poems of the Holocaust
    Pterodactyl Rose: Poems of Ecology
    Ribbons: The Gulf War — A Poem
    The Host: Selected Poems 1965-1990

TED HIRSCHFIELD
 German Requiem: Poems of the War and the Atonement of a Third Reich Child

VIRGINIA V. JAMES HLAVSA
 Waking October Leaves: Reanimations by a Small-Town Girl

RODGER KAMENETZ
 The Missing Jew: New and Selected Poems

NORBERT KRAPF
 Somewhere in Southern Indiana: Poems of Midwestern Origins

ADRIAN C. LOUIS
 Blood Thirsty Savages

JOSEPH MEREDITH
 Hunter's Moon: Poems from Boyhood to Manhood

TIME BEING BOOKS®
POETRY IN SIGHT AND SOUND

FOR OUR FREE CATALOG OR TO ORDER

(800) 331-6605 Monday through Friday
8 a.m. to 4 p.m. Central time
FAX: (314) 432-7939

DATE DUE			
5-10-21			

#47-0108 Peel Off Pressure Sensitive

DISCARD

Mt. Juliet
High School Library